Sir George Etherege

Twayne's English Authors Series

Bertram H. Davis, Editor

Florida State University

TEAS 446

THE

WORKS

OF

Sir George Etherege:

Containing His

PLAYS

AND

POEMS.

LONDON,

Printed for *H. H.* And Sold by *J. Tonson*, within *Grays-Inn* Gate, next *Grays-Inn* Lane; and *T. Bennet*, at the *Half-Moon* in St. *Paul's* Church-yard. 1704.

Title page of the first collected edition

Sir George Etherege

By Arthur R. Huseboe

Augustana College

Twayne Publishers
A Division of G.K. Hall & Co. • Boston

Sir George Etherege

Arthur R. Huseboe

Published by Twayne Publishers
A Division of G.K. Hall & Co.
70 Lincoln Street
Boston, Massachusetts 02111

Copyediting supervised by Lewis DeSimone
Book production by Marne Sultz
Book design by Barbara Anderson

Typeset in 11 pt. Garamond
by P&M Typesetting, Waterbury, Connecticut

Printed on permanent/durable acid-free paper
and bound in the United States of America

Library of Congress Cataloging in Publication Data

Huseboe, Arthur R., 1931–
Sir George Etherege.

(Twayne's English authors series ; TEAS 446)
Bibliography: p. 130
Includes index.
1. Etherege, George, Sir, 1635?–1691. 2. Authors, English—Early modern, 1500–1700—Biography. I. Title. II. Series.
PR3432.Z5H8 1987 822′.4 [B] 86-29581
ISBN 0-8057-6946-3

For Doris Louise,
my wife,
and Frederick Manfred,
my companyero

Contents

About the Author

Arthur R. Huseboe is professor of English and chairman of the Humanities Division at Augustana College (Sioux Falls, South Dakota). His B. A. degree is from that institution; his M. A. is from the University of South Dakota; and his Ph.D. is from Indiana University, where he wrote a dissertation on Alexander Pope under the guidance of the late Irvin Ehrenpreis.

Professor Huseboe has published articles about Etherege in *Notes and Queries, Modern Philology,* and the collection *Studies in English and American Literature* (1978). His book *Sir John Vanbrugh* was published in 1976 in Twayne's English Authors Series, and his monograph on Herbert Krause appeared in the Western Writers Series (Boise State University, 1985).

Professor Huseboe is presently at work on an edition of the selected letters of American novelist Frederick Manfred. He is currently directing a three-year program, funded by the Andrew W. Mellon Foundation, to strengthen the teaching of the humanities in northern plains high schools.

Preface

Sir George Etherege's life and career are much better known to us today than ever before, principally because of the work of Professor Dorothy Foster in the 1920s and Professor Frederick Bracher in the recent past. Their several biographical studies have proven to be invaluable to me in the writing of this book. The playwright-poet who charmed London audiences with popular and influential comedies in the 1660s and 1670s is no longer the shadowy figure that he had become even before his death in 1692, and it is at last possible to write a detailed and accurate biography about him.

The present study is intended to supply the need for a compact introduction to the life and career of an important Restoration playwright, poet, and letter writer. All but one of the book-length studies of Etherege that have been written to date have been master's theses or doctoral dissertations. The one published book, Dale Underwood's study (1957), is an influential examination of the intellectual background of Etherege's plays, but it does not profess to be biography nor does it deal with Etherege the poet and letter writer. The most ambitious by far of the dissertations is that by Mme N. J. Rigaud: *George Etherege, Dramaturge de la Restauration Anglaise* (1980). Nobody else has read so very many Jacobean and Restoration comedies in order to search for echoes and analogues in Etherege's plays, and no one else has brought together so much Etheregeana as she. It is unfortunate for scholars that she has no plans to prepare an English translation.

There have been, of course, a great many shorter works on Etherege, as is borne out by Professor David Mann's indispensable reference guide (1980). The present critical biography draws on a number of these in order to provide the first book-length examination of both Etherege's life and his works. In chapter 1, I have assembled material from a wide range of sources in order to present a picture of the playwright's life in Maidenhead and London, including sketches of his friends and members of his family. Unhappily, I have not been able to find the date of Etherege's birth, for the transcripts and original registers for Bray Parish (which included his parents' home, Maidenhead) do not exist after 1635, the year that George's older sister Anne was born there. I have also searched a number of London parish registers on the chance that Etherege or others in the family might have been born in London when Captain Etherege served as purveyor to the queen. No evidence of such births was found in the registers of St. Clement Danes, St. Martin-in-the-Fields, St. Mary-le-Strand, St. Margaret, Westminster, or Westminster Abbey.

Some years ago, however, I was fortunate enough to discover new information about Etherege's maternal family in the registers of Bray Parish, and I have incorporated some of that material here. In addition, I was recently able to read the will of Christopher Newstead, Etherege's stepfather. From it I learned that the playwright's mother was not left in poverty at her husband's death, as formerly reported. Hence, it was not necessary for Etherege to write in order to support her, although his small inheritance probably led him to write in order to improve his own situation. Finally, I have added to our knowledge of Etherege's law career at Clement's Inn by naming the principal there, John Grene, and the young men who were enrolled about the same time.

In bringing together everything known about Etherege's immediate family, including my own discoveries about his maternal relatives, I am able in chapter 1 to point out similarities between his early life and events and characters in the plays. In chapters 2 through 5, the analyses of Etherege's plays, poems, and letters, I am able to offer some new interpretations in addition to reviewing a number of earlier ones.

The present study makes no attempt to redeem Etherege's poetry from centuries of neglect but does argue that his letters deserve more attention. Most of the poetry is of little moment. Apart from the conventional love poems and the songs in the plays, there are the bawdy rambles and satires that have much of the same spice as the wit in the comedies. Were it not for those comedies, however, poet Etherege would have, one suspects, only antiquarian interest. As a letter writer, on the other hand, he was a skilled prose stylist and a keen observer. Sybil Rosenfeld's *Letterbook* and Frederick Bracher's *Letters* are the essential collections for further study of his epistolary style; I have been able to add a little to their discoveries.

I have endeavored throughout the book to combine biography and literary criticism in a way that has not been done before for Etherege. The plays benefit by being read against the circumstances and persons that are an intimate part of Sir George Etherege's life, and I have treated the three of them principally as comedies of character. So as to assist the reader who is not familiar with the plays, I have provided a substantial synopsis of each. Throughout *Sir George Etherege* all passages quoted from the plays are from the recent modern-spelling edition by Michael Cordner (1982).

Of the many debts that I owe in the writing of this book, the greatest is to Professor Frederick Bracher. His scholarly work has been invaluable, and his letters to me over several years have helped me draw a clearer picture of Etherege the man. Bracher was also kind enough to read an early draft of chapter 1 and to suggest directions for further investigations. Also helpful, but at a much greater distance, has been Miss Pamela Stewart, assistant archivist in the Diocesan Record Office, Salisbury, England. She was able to provide me with information from the parish registers of Old Windsor relating to the family of Etherege's mother, Mary Powney. I am extremely grateful to both of them. Others helped me directly with valuable information: Professor Donald Sutherland (University of Iowa) helped decipher the entries in the Clement's Inn Admissions Book; K. C. Harrison, the Westminster City Librarian, searched parish registers in London; Hubert Chesshyre (Chester Herald of Arms) and Conrad Swan (York Herald of Arms) ransacked the records—to no avail—for information about Etherege's knighting; John Bultena unraveled some knotty legal terminology; and the librarians of the public library at Maidenhead supplied me—on interlibrary loan—with copies of J. Wesley Walker's *History* and other useful materials.

The roots of this study go back many years, and I owe a debt of gratitude to three men who stimulated my interest in the seventeenth and eighteenth centuries. Professor Donald Baker (University of Colorado) taught courses on those two centuries at the University of South Dakota. The late Professor Irvin Ehrenpreis (University of Virginia) guided my dissertation on Alexander Pope at Indiana University. And Professor Robert C. Steensma (University of Utah) first suggested to me a book in the Twayne Series.

Much of my research was done while on a leave of absence from Augustana College, and I am grateful to the administration and to my colleagues in the English department for their support. A number of grants have been helpful as well, from the Augustana Faculty Studies and Research Committee and the Bush Committee, from the National Endowment for the Humanities, from the American Philosophical Society, and from the Board of College Education (ALC).

Several libraries and archives have been especially cooperative: the British Library (British Museum), the Public Record Office, the Wilson Library at the University of Minnesota, the Houghton Library at Harvard University, the University of South Dakota Library, and the Mikkelsen Library at Augustana College.

Special thanks must go to my typist, Mrs. Marilyn Berry, assisted by Mrs. Glenna Swier, and to my wife, Doris, who assisted in preparing the bibliography for this book. Their help was indispensable.

Arthur R. Huseboe

Augustana College

Chronology

1634 7 October: Captain George Etherege marries Mary Powney.

1635 July: their daughter Anne Etherege is baptized.

1636 Likely year of birth of George Etherege, the future playwright. October: his father buys the office of purveyor to Queen Henrietta Maria.

1644 The queen flees to France and Captain Etherege probably follows.

1650 29 September: Captain Etherege dies in France, leaving seven children.

1652 George Etherege's mother marries widower Christopher Newstead.

1654 Etherege is apprenticed to attorney George Gosnold of Beaconsfield.

1656 Beginning of lawsuit relating to Etherege's inheritance. His signature starts to turn up as witness to Gosnold's signature; he lives for a time in London, perhaps on business for Gosnold.

1657 10 December: Judge Chaloner Chute decides the family lawsuit in Etherege's favor.

1658 March or April: Grandfather Etherege dies and George becomes heir to lands in Kent worth £40 a year.

1659 19 February: admitted to Clement's Inn to study law.

1662 About this year Etherege's bawdy verse "The Imperfect Enjoyment" begins to circulate. His stepfather Christopher Newstead dies.

1663 Etherege becomes acquainted with the young Lord Buckhurst (later earl of Dorset).

1664 March: probable month of the premier performance of *The Comical Revenge* at the Duke's Playhouse, more successful than any previous comedy. 8 July: licensed for the press; published shortly after for Henry Herringman.

1665 March: by this month his poem "To Her Excellence the Marchioness of Newcastle" is circulating.

1667 His first poem to appear in print, "To a Lady, Asking Him How Long He Would Love Her," is published in the miscellany *Catch that Catch Can*. 12 August: Grandfather Richard Powney dies.

1668 6 February: *She Would If She Could* opens at the Duke's Playhouse; Pepys reports on Etherege's disappointment at the poor acting. 18 May: Charles Sedley's *The Mulberry-Garden* opens at Drury Lane with a character named Estridge in it. 24 June: *She Would If She Could* is licensed for the press; printed for Henry Herringman soon after. 31 July: Etherege is sworn a Gentleman of the Privy Chamber in Ordinary. 15 August: goes to Constantinople as secretary to Sir Daniel Harvey.

1669 Three of his poems are printed in *The New Academy of Complements*.

1671 1 May: by now Etherege has left Constantinople and is in Paris. 9 November: "A Prologue Spoken at the Opening of the Duke's New Playhouse" in Dorset Garden.

1672 Nine of his verses are printed in *A Collection of Poems*.

1673 Acts as witness to the earlier knighting of his cousin Sir William Paul.

1676 11 March: *The Man of Mode* at the Dorset Garden Theatre; 3 June: licensed; printed soon after. 18 June: involved with Lord Rochester and others in a squabble with the watch at Epsom.

1679 Knighted, probably late in the year; married soon after.

1680 14 January: Charles Hatton reports him "very dangerously hurt" on this date when a tennis court collapses.

1682 29 September: listed as one of the duke of York's pensioners at £100 per year.

1685 March: a warrant is issued directed to Etherege, "whom his Maj. has thought fit to employ in his service in Germany." 21 November: arrives in Ratisbon (Regensburg).

1686 19 January and 29 April: verse letters to Lord Middleton.

1687 16 February: Dryden calls Etherege "the undoubted best author" of English prose.

1688 23 December: James II leaves England.

1689 18 January: Etherege receives word that King James has arrived in Paris. Leaves shortly after to join him.

	28 September: date of Etherege's last known letters from Paris, to his wife, his sister, and a money lender.
1691	Rumors of Etherege's death in Paris.
1692	10 May: "Sr. George Etherege dyed without Issue," according to testimony by his nephew George Etherege.

Chapter One
Life and Times

From the vantage point of the twentieth century the life of Sir George Etherege looks to us a good deal like a long and dim tunnel, with a brightly lighted side passage near the beginning and another near the end, each leading off into an enormous room that is filled with the most entertaining company imaginable. Regarding the main part of Etherege's life, however, we know very little; even the exact dates of his birth and death are uncertain. Those two side passages, times in Etherege's life about which much is now known, have been illuminated by the discovery in 1880 by Sir Edmund Gosse and Edward Scott of the Ratisbon letterbook and by the examination in the 1920s by Dorothy Foster of a lengthy family lawsuit. Together, these materials have supplied more information concerning Etherege's youth and middle age than is known about comparable periods in the life of any other Restoration comic playwright.[1]

Moreover, Frederick Bracher's publication in 1974 of new letters from the Harvard letterbooks and Middleton papers and of new facts about Etherege in Ratisbon (Regensburg), Germany, has greatly increased our understanding of Sir George's last years. And Bracher's printing in 1980 of an article about George's legal training has provided valuable new information about his youth. It can now be claimed that only Samuel Pepys, among all of Etherege's literary contemporaries, is more familiar to us in those personal details of diet, disease, and dress that make the difference between the shadow and the man.

The 1656–57 lawsuit material uncovered by Foster reveals much about the relatives and friends who touched at so many points the life of the twenty-year-old George Etherege, law clerk and playwright-to-be. From the testimony that fills the manuscript pages of interrogatory and deposition emerge the three central figures in the litigation and in the playwright's early life. First, Grandfather George Etherege, infirm and bitter but in his prime a pillar of fatherly concern, willing to bear for a dozen years the burden of supporting his eldest son's numerous orphans. Then, that eldest son, Captain George Etherege, the playwright's father, for a time the manager of Grandfather Etherege's plantation in the Bermudas, later the holder of a minor office at court but leaving an impecunious widow and seven children at his death in 1650. Finally, standing out from the pages of questions and answers and etched in black, as it were, is the villain of the piece. He is the playwright's uncle, John Etherege, divine of Tangmer, Sussex, and the source of much of Grandfather Etherege's grief and anger.

Scattered throughout the pages of testimony delivered at the Bull Inn in Maidenhead, Berkshire, are vignettes of others in the Etherege circle: young George's mother, Mary Powney, the daughter of a substantial gentleman of neighboring Old Windsor; several of George's brothers and sisters; and Mary's second husband, Christopher Newstead, the controversial chaplain of Maidenhead. Not the least of the portraits that take shape out of the lawsuit material are those of such acquaintances as Thomas Cherry, the harried mercer of Maidenhead and young George's great-uncle, who had to be coaxed twice before he would come on a busy market day to be a witness in the suit; and Grandfather Etherege's servant, Grace Luckins, whose outspoken opinions and perpetual meddling in her master's affairs made her a likely model for the playwright to use when he created Sentry in *She Would If She Could* and Pert in *The Man of Mode*.

Antecedents

Before Professor Foster's ransacking of the Public Record Office, only a few scraps of information about Sir George's family existed. He was thought by Charles Gildon to be of an Oxfordshire family[2] and by William Oldys to be related to Dr. George Etheridge, Regius Professor of Greek at Oxford in the late sixteenth century.[3] These connections, however, have not been confirmed. The future playwright's paternal family has been traced directly only to his great-grandfather George of London and his grandfather George (1576–1658), a wealthy vintner, an investor in the Virginia and Somers Islands Companies, and later a well-to-do leaseholder in Maidenhead and a landholder in Kent.[4] The marriage of Grandfather George Etherege in about 1606 resulted in five children, all born in London. Their dates of baptism are recorded in the St. Clement Danes parish register as follows: George, father of the playwright, baptized 11 August 1607; Martha, baptized 24 February 1609; John, baptized 15

April 1610; and Mary, baptized on 19 September 1613. The burial of the infant Mary is noted in the parish register on 28 September 1614, as is that of Charles (whose date of baptism is not given) on 28 July 1617.

Throughout these years in London Grandfather Etherege prospered. The profits from his wine business he invested in the reorganized Virginia Company (1609) and later in the Bermuda Islands, or Somers Islands, Company (1615). His name appears with 658 others in the charter of the Virginia Company as "George Etheridge, gentleman," and he was frequently in attendance at London meetings of the company, as the records show, especially after the 1622 Virginia massacre and the bitter controversies that followed. The dissolution of the company by King James in 1625 in order to end its perpetual squabbling may have had adverse financial effects for Etherege, but by then he was already among the 118 original investors in a company formed to settle Bermuda, "That happy island," as Edmund Waller wrote,

> where huge lemons grow,
> And orange trees, which golden fruit do bear,
> The Hesperian garden boasts of none so fair;
> Where shining pearl, coral, and many a pound,
> On the rich shore, of ambergris is found.
> "The Battle of the Summer Islands"

For the first years Grandfather Etherege's investment in four shares in Lord Paget's tract of land or "Tribe" seems to have prospered, with good relations existing between tenants and shareholders and a handsome income coming to him of some forty pounds a year. On at least one occasion he shared in the exotic treasures of Waller's "rich shore" when "9 ounces of Ambergreece [were] found floating within the bounds of Mr. Etheridge his land." But with time, as letters from the company show, increasing commerce brought problems: foreign ships and even English ships with no company connections were selling provisions in the islands and carrying back valuable cargoes of the best tobacco; the owners' profits, it was averred, were being eaten up by excessive charges made by the tenants, and attempts to cultivate mulberry trees for silk producing were proving unsuccessful. Affairs needed to be managed at closer hand, and so in about 1627 Grandfather Etherege's son George, now in his twenty-first year and styled "Captain," was sent off to manage the Bermuda lands.

For nearly seven years Captain Etherege oversaw the development of his father's ninety-eight acres, with but two journeys home until his final return. The record of a council meeting in 1630 reveals a little of the captain's dealings—in pounds of tobacco—with his two tenants, Captain Jennings and John Brookes. In January 1631 he demonstrated his loyalty to the king (and to the Somers Islands Company) by testifying that he had overheard the master of the ship *Tyger,* one Captain John Rose, boast "that he would steal coustome of Tobacco in despight of his Majesties teeth and his coustomers." At the council's command the *Tyger* returned to England without its indiscreet and dishonest master. Little of importance beyond these notices is known of Captain Etherege's stay in the islands, and by the spring of 1634 he was back in England, rich in experience certainly, but not much improved financially and still under the control of his strong-willed father.

Apart from the troubles in the Virginia Company, the fortunes of Grandfather Etherege continued to advance. In 1625 he inherited from his brother-in-law, John Rixman,[5] a valuable half share in the profits of the lease of the manor of Ives, or Ivy, in Maidenhead, Berkshire, and was later able to buy the remaining share from his cousin William Middleton. In 1626 Etherege managed to place his troublesome younger son John with a London glass-seller, where he hoped the wayward boy would learn to become self-sufficient. And in early 1628 he arranged an excellent match for his daughter Martha: she was married—in the same parish church where she had been christened—to William Canning, the eldest son of William Canning, Senior, deputy governor of the Bermuda Islands Company and a wealthy London merchant. In that same year that saw all his children apparently settled, however, the elder Etherege made a decision that would eventually bring him, in his own words, "with sorrow to the grave," and that would have a lasting effect on the life of his grandson and heir, the playwright-to-be: the elder Etherege bought, in the names of his sons, two farms in Kent worth forty pounds a year.

Early in his negotiations with Points and Uranious Morrice, Etherege discovered that there were judgments against the Kent land, and on the advice of his attorney determined to protect himself by taking the property in the name of his eldest son. Since Captain Etherege was in the Bermudas at the time, however, and "it was uncertain whether [he] was living or not," attorney Mallet advised further that the name of the younger son John be added to the conveyance so that the premises would pass to a person who would "execute the trust thereof as [the elder Etherege] should direct." It was a clumsy arrangement, made even clumsier by the fact that a few months later Grandfather Etherege was required, according to the terms of John Rixman's will, to pay out fifty pounds to each of his three children. Eighteen years later, when the future playwright was named as heir, John was to charge bitterly that he had seen none of the Rixman legacy, that his father had not paid him the money but had used it in the purchase of the Kent properties.

By the spring of 1634 and Captain Etherege's return from the Bermudas, the elder George Etherege seems to have retired from the London wine trade[6] and was well established in the Thames village of Maidenhead, close to the Manor of Ives, from which he was now receiving one hundred pounds rent. Here in Maidenhead his son George met and shortly married Mary, the twenty-two-year-old daughter of Richard Powney, gentleman of nearby Old Windsor. It may be that the two fathers had been talking of a match between their children for some time, since their acquaintance dated from 1632. The marriage arrangement that they worked out was, at any rate, a handsome one: Powney agreed to give an outright dowry of five hundred pounds, and Etherege would provide thirty pounds a year to the couple for ten years and would settle on his son and the children of the match property worth over sixty-six pounds per year. The wedding took place on Tuesday, 7 October 1634, at Bray Parish Church.[7]

For the first year of their married life Captain Etherege and wife lived with his father, but not entirely happily it seems. Having arranged an advantageous marriage, the elder Etherege was reluctant to do any more for his oldest son, even charging the newlyweds forty pounds for their board and room. It had made her husband "very melancholly," said Mary many years later, for living with her father-in-law cost the couple more than the annual amount he was providing them according to the terms of the agreement with her father. To a man of Captain Etherege's experience, who had lived independently for seven years while managing his father's Bermudas land, the demand for payment must have seemed especially unreasonable. Nor would it have relieved his gloom could he have known that the elder George Etherege was now giving forty pounds a year to his scapegrace younger son John, who had been apprenticed to four masters in eight years and had left all of them, who had run into such debt by "his unsettled and improvident courses" that his father had had to rescue him, and who now had married a woman of no estate and against his father's will.

Where Captain George and Mary Etherege moved in 1635, whether elsewhere in Maidenhead or to another town, is not known. The christening of their first child, Anne, is recorded in the Bray parish register for July 1635,[8] but the register beyond this date is no longer extant and the intriguing question remains as to when and where young George, the future playwright, and the other five children were born. From the 1657 lawsuit and from his given name we know that he was the eldest son of the couple. Contemporary references to Sir George Etherege's birth by William Oldys and John Dryden indicate that he was born by 1636 and thus would have followed Anne as the second child in the family.[9] Moreover, according to seventeenth-century practice, aspiring attorneys were "placed" at about age eighteen; it is significant that Etherege was placed with attorney George Gosnold in 1654, eighteen years after 1636. Anne's birth in the summer of 1635 would put George's birthday no earlier than the spring of 1636. Since John was apprenticed in 1655 and Margaret in 1656, they were very likely the third and fourth children in order. We have no information to indicate when Richard, Elizabeth, and the unnamed child may have been born.[10]

Disrupted Family Life

Sometime in 1636 Captain George Etherege took a step that changed his situation as significantly as his voyage to the New World or his marriage: he bought a place at court worth two hundred pounds and—so it would appear—was required to travel frequently to London. The position was that of purveyor to Queen Henrietta Maria, and in order to make the purchase he used three hundred pounds of his wife's marriage portion and the three hundred pounds that the elder Etherege had promised to pay over a ten-year period.[11]

While an income of two hundred pounds a year was handsome indeed, journeying to, from, and about London was not without its hazards. The worst plague in eleven years had struck the city that summer, an attack so bad that the playhouses were closed for the next eighteen months.[12] The position, too, carried with it peculiar risks, for purveyors—even more than tax collectors—suffered nearly universal distrust and even hatred, and in the very year of Captain Etherege's purchase their office had been newly regulated because of dissatisfaction with their activities.[13] With other officers in the same occupation, Captain Etherege had the prerogative of purchasing provisions and other goods for the royal household at bargain rates and in preference to all other customers. It was inevitable that the system would be abused, and some purveyors were notorious for the ingenuity by which they lined their own pockets, including the obvious device of appropriating more goods than were ultimately delivered to the bakeries and butteries of Whitehall.

For the rest of his life Captain Etherege held the lucrative but despised office, if we can so interpret the Eighth Interrogatory at the 1657 trial, and he probably accompanied the queen's entourage to France in 1644, continuing in her service in some capacity until his death there in September 1650.[14] How closely the family may have been connected with the court from 1636 to 1642, whether young George ever accompanied his father to Whitehall, and what effect such supposed visits may have had on his later actions and attitudes are beyond reasonable speculation. But the queen was not popular with Englishmen in the 1630s—and never had been—and her aggressive Catholicism and the rash of well-publicized conversions in those years were compounded by her subjects' suspicions of her French origins and of her influence over the king. Something of that unpopularity would have been conveyed to young George whether or not there had been such visits.

Captain Etherege's place at court and the birth of his son in 1636 came at the beginning of that peculiar period of domestic and foreign tranquillity in English history that has been labeled by C. V. Wedgwood "The King's Peace." From 1629 until 1640 King Charles I ruled without Parliament. It was an experiment in personal government that turned out to be the last gasp of royal absolutism, but for a time it appeared that Parliament might indeed be dead and that Charles could manage to patch together a workable foreign policy and to organize the Church and the economy at home. The seeds for the coming rebellion were already sown, however, and nowhere did they sprout with more vigor than in Scotland, where William Laud's efforts to strengthen the Anglican church were noisily protested. The resistance grew at length into the National Covenant in 1638 and the declaration of Presbyterianism as the Scots' official religion.

The king's efforts to solve by arms the problem in the north led to a series of embarrassing defeats and the Treaty of Berwick (June 1639), a breathing space until he could summon a parliament that would help him mobilize the country. Instead of mutely voting for the necessary legislation to conduct a successful war with Scotland, however, this first parliament in eleven years launched into what the king could only construe as an orgy of debate over his conduct of recent state business. English liberties were of greater concern to the members than an uneasy northern border, and when the king was threatened with a petition to end the campaign, the Short Parliament—as it was immediately dubbed—was dissolved. That spring the Scots took Newcastle upon Tyne. By fall there were mass demonstrations in London demanding a parliament, and with money gone and the Scots in possession of large chunks of English land, Charles gave in. In November 1640 the fifth parliament of his reign assembled. It was to be his last.

The events of 1641 and 1642 had a catastrophic effect on the life and career of Captain George Etherege and his family, as indeed they had on the lives of tens of thousands of Englishmen. Sometime before the autumn of 1642, with his task of providing provisions for the queen's household made nearly impossible by the economic paralysis that had struck London and was spreading into the countryside, Captain Etherege probably arranged to have his family supported by Grandfather Etherege. The best knowledge we have of this likelihood is the testimony in 1657 of the servant Grace Luckins that Grandfather Etherege had supported Mary and the children "att greate cost and chardges, ever since their Father's decease and for many years before"; and the testimony of Richard Powney, Mary's father, that Captain Etherege's income of about two hundred pounds per year had continued until the time of "the troubles," that is, until 1642.[15] Nevertheless, the events that led to the king's declaration of war on 22 August 1642 were unmistakable signs that the court was in immediate danger from mobs without and decay within, and prudence would have dictated that Captain Etherege make some such preparations.

The Catholicism of the court and a universal fear among English citizens of a Catholic uprising were the sources of greatest danger to Captain Etherege in 1642. In the previous October the slaughter of Protestants during the Ulster Rebellion had created a panic in London and in many parts of the counties. In November 1641 the House of Commons heard reports of far-ranging Catholic plots to mount an army and to kill 108 members of Parliament, and the great myth of a worldwide papist conspiracy to destroy England seemed confirmed.

The House of Commons in response issued the first of what Sir George Etherege was many years later to call "the infamous Remonstrances of our Rebellious Parliament."[16]

When in December mobs rioted at the House of Lords and the Commons impeached the bishops there, the rumor followed that they were about to impeach the queen as well. King Charles attempted the arrest of the five leaders on 5 January 1642, going to Commons in person. Panic swept London, spreading quickly to Buckinghamshire, where several thousand men marched on London two days later to rescue their threatened parliament man, John Hampden. On 10 January the king fled with his family to Hampton Court, and the great administrative system of which Captain Etherege was a part began breaking down. Throughout January and February thousands of poor people from the city and petitioners from the counties milled and marched about the Houses of Parliament and Whitehall, protesting the "evil counsellors" surrounding the king, pleading for bread, complaining of the collapse of trade and demonstrating—above all—against the papists. By spring the exodus of courtiers was underway, each man having to choose whether to obey the summons and follow his sovereign to York or to remain in the capital in an attempt to hold the machine of government together.[17] By October a melancholy Royalist pamphleteer could regret the vast emptiness of the abandoned palace, where "now there's nothing but the raw sent of moist walls, and all as silent as midnight."[18]

Exactly when Captain George Etherege left England is not known. That he remained loyal to the Royalist cause, however, is borne out by the fact that he remained as purveyor until his death and by the label "rebell" attached to him fifteen years later by his brother John. In February 1642 the queen hurried to France, returning in a year without the troops she had sought. After several months with Charles at Oxford, however, with war raging on all sides, she fled again to France and there undertook in every way possible to support the king's campaign until his execution in 1649. Since Captain Etherege is said to have held his office during his lifetime and since he died in France on 29 September 1650, it is probable that he followed his sovereign there, leaving his family behind in Grandfather Etherege's capable hands.

It may be that young George spent some time abroad with his father. His first play, *The Comical Revenge* (1664), is evidence that he was by then at least on good terms with the French language, and the later two plays and his letters reflect a knowledge of Paris and a mastery of the language. But the tradition that he was educated at the Thame grammar school, and the speculation that he attended Cambridge briefly and traveled into France and Flanders when he was very young[19] have not yet been supported by any existing evidence. What seems more likely is that his education was by tutor or in school at Maidenhead until he was old enough to be placed with Gosnold at Beaconsfield, where he might at least learn Law-French as a beginning of his acquaintance with that language. He would have had occasion to perfect it later on, when he studied law at Clement's Inn in London.

Family Circle

The circle of relatives and family friends in which young George Etherege grew to manhood is a richly varied one, and our knowledge of their life in Maidenhead during the troubled times from 1642 until the Restoration is remarkably full, thanks to the extensive lawsuit material discovered by Professor Foster. And while it is pleasant to dispel much of the mystery surrounding the playwright's life, as we now can do, that knowledge can also give us valuable insights into some of Etherege's stage characters and situations. It should be no surprise to find that, like other playwrights, George Etherege often wrote best about people he knew best, both from his observations at home and those in London and at Court.

Young George was strongly influenced, certainly, by Grandfather Etherege, although from time to time one or another of the seven children of Captain Etherege was cared for by Grandfather Powney and later on by Mary and her second husband. In his later years Sir George wrote to his brother Richard and to his nephew and his mother, but the only member of the family to whom he makes direct reference in his extant correspondence is to his grandfather Etherege.[20] The character of Lord Bevill in *The Comical Revenge,* in particular in his insistence upon filial obedience, certainly seems to owe a good deal to the elder Etherege—of whom his son John said, "his father was so severe that he dared not withstand him, so veiled obedience."[21] Like Grandfather Etherege, too, whose wife is nowhere mentioned in the documents, Bevill appears to be a widower. That the elder Etherege grew more conciliatory as he advanced in years is apparent from his efforts to pacify his son John and at the same time to keep his agreement with Richard Powney to provide an estate for Captain Etherege's children. But he was then nearing eighty and it is not likely that young George had him in mind when he created the accommodating, but otherwise unattractive, Sir Oliver Cockwood.

From the time he was six until he was eighteen, young George and his brothers and sisters grew up under the influence of two women. Of his mother we know relatively little. She bore seven children in rapid succession before her husband's exile, and reared them to adulthood with only an aging father-in-law providing much help. At Captain Etherege's death it was painfully clear that there could no longer be any hope that her precarious financial situation would soon improve, and after mourning for the traditional year—and a little more—she married again and was thereafter able to ease the burden of Grandfather Etherege, now in his mid-seventies. If Sir George was fond of his mother, it may be that he gave some of her traits to Widow Rich, the widow in *The Comical Revenge* and the only widow in any of the plays. Widow Rich is a wealthy, witty, and attractive noblewoman, sister to Lord Bevill and in love with the rake-hero Sir Frederick Frollick. To go the final step in this chain of speculation means that if Sir Frederick is either the subconscious projection of Etherege himself or, as Gosse believed, a deliberate self-portrait, then Sir George has created for his dramatic alter ego an appealing mistress modeled after his own mother.

About Grace Luckins, Grandfather Etherege's longtime spinster maidservant, young George ought to have had a rather more ambivalent attitude. From her testimony at the 1657 hearings it is clear that she was Grandfather Etherege's only household servant and that she had been so for many years. Sir George remembered her with affection in Germany some thirty years later when he wished a friend in England "a merry Christmas, and as good a stomach to the Plumbroth as an old servant of my Grandfather's had, whose onely grace all the good time was 'God love me as I love Plum pottage' " (*Letters,* 163). But Grace Luckins was also a meddler in family affairs, jealous of the favoritism shown Captain Etherege's children and eager to see John reinstated in his father's affections. It was she who urged the old man to "do something for John" and who secretly sent for the younger son during Grandfather Etherege's illness in 1654, telling John the Kent properties were in his name; and it was she who testified later that she had overheard Grandfather Etherege promise to deed the Kent properties to John at his death rather than to young George and the other children.

The playwright's "revenge" for this disloyalty was to use the occasion of his first comedy to give her name to Wheadle's mistress, Grace, the whore whom Sir Frederick Frollick has been annoying as *The Comical Revenge* opens. The similarity of the name Grace to that of the heroic and beautiful Graciana may be mere coincidence, of course, or it may instead reflect Etherege's mixed feelings of affection and dislike for his grandfather's maidservant. At all odds, the character of Mrs. Grace is scandalous and the choice of name seems to be an intentional—if very private—form of punishment. In the later plays, on the other hand, Etherege certainly included some of Grace Luckins's traits in two characters in whom he had little emotional investment: both Sentry and Pert are outspoken busybodies, bold enough to treat their mistresses like familiars and active in their affairs, and in general possessing those qualities that appear from the documents to have been Grace's.

Of the brothers and sisters who grew up with George in Maidenhead there is little to indicate their relationships with the future playwright or what characters in the comedies, if any, may have embodied their traits. The two younger girls, Margaret and Elizabeth, may have served to some extent as models for the two sets of sisters prominent in both *The Comical Revenge* and *She Would If She Could*. And Margaret's placement in 1656 with Mr. Castle, a sempster in the New Exchange, was undoubtedly the source of some elements in the scene that Etherege set in "that arsenal of choice vanities"[22] in his second play. Brother John, too, was placed in an occupation that figures in the three comedies at several points, but that apprenticeship to a surgeon was for little more than a year, ending with his death at sea or in the East Indies not long after his placing in 1655. The references to medicine in the comedies are no more than might be expected of any playwright with an ordinary knowledge of the profession.

Outside of Etherege's immediate family were events and people that very likely had a discernible influence upon his character and writing. The feelings of insecurity that must have followed his father's exile were heightened by the tragic happenings of the Civil War, many of which impinged on life in Maidenhead. Three in particular—the last interview of King Charles with his children, his execution, and the news of Captain Etherege's death in France—came in rapid succession and were almost, but not quite, the capstones to a long series of events that contributed heavily to the sense of personal isolation and the air of deep disillusionment that are so evident in Etherege's plays.

George Etherege was a boy of only ten when Charles I and his children were permitted by Parliament to meet for the last time, on a July day in Maidenhead, first at St. Mary's Church and later—after riding through streets strewn with flowers and greenery—in the Greyhound Inn.[23] But the stories that George heard of that melancholy parting near at hand in 1647 and the even more disturbing news of the king's execution in London eighteen months later were not as profoundly shocking as the word that reached the family in October 1650 of Captain Etherege's death in France on 29 September. If young George—then thirteen or fourteen—had been abroad with Captain Etherege during the years just before 1650, the loss of his father would have further strengthened his sense of isolation and his hatred of the Puritan regime that had been responsible for their exile in the first place. But the only hint, beyond the slender speculations of Oldys and others that he had traveled and perhaps studied in France, is the testimony of Christopher Newstead in 1657 regarding the whereabouts of four of the seven Etherege children a little over a year after their father's death.[24] Even if the Etherege child unnamed in the testimony had died in the interval between Captain Etherege's death and his widow's remarriage in early 1652, there are still two children to account for, and some part of the explanation of their location might very well include a stay in France for young George after his father's death.

With the children growing to adulthood in the 1650s, the breakup of the Etherege family was inevitable, but it was speeded up by Mary's marriage in 1652 to Christopher Newstead, a fifty-nine-year-old widower and the controversial chaplain at Maidenhead since 1650. He had come to the position under suspicion of Royalist leanings: his appointment in 1642 to the rectory of Stisted in Essex had been held up by the House of Lords, and when it was finally confirmed, the parishioners refused to let him obtain possession or to preach. In 1644 or 1645 Newstead was sequestered (deprived of his benefice), although one-fifth of the profits of the rectory were granted to his first wife, Mary Fulhurst; and his later appointment to the chapel of Maidenhead was opposed by the Committee of Approbation of Public Preachers, who questioned "his submission to the present

Government and fitness to preach."[25] A fair share of the animosity directed against Newstead came because the unpopular Archbishop William Laud had nominated him to Stisted. Laud had done so as a favor to Sir Thomas Roe, whom Newstead had served as chaplain. Until Laud's execution in early 1645, he had rolled up a great stockpile of ill will among Scottish Presbyterians and English Puritans for his vigorous efforts to impose Anglican orthodoxy upon both countries. How much of that antipathy was Newstead's inheritance can only be estimated, but he continued to be watched throughout his years at Maidenhead, preaching for a time by special permission of Cromwell's council of state, and free of Puritan surveillance only with the restoration of the monarchy.

Such Royalist connections in Mary's new husband were not entirely unwelcome to Grandfather Etherege, whose eldest son had been in the service of the deposed queen and in whose household Christmas continued to be celebrated in the hearty way that so annoyed the Puritans. Newstead could boast as well a brief term as chaplain extraordinary to the king (1641) and a long association as chaplain to the greatest of all statesmen under James I and Charles I, Sir Thomas Roe (c. 1581–1644), emissary to the great mogul Jehangir, ambassador to the Ottoman Porte, Constantinople, and treaty-maker without peer.[26] From his stepfather young George must have heard at some time of Newstead's years in Turkey (1621–1628), then as remote to Englishmen as the Bermuda Islands were, including a sea fight with Maltese galleys on the return voyage. Etherege's appointment in 1668 as secretary to Sir Daniel Harvey in Constantinople must have appeared to him a striking coincidence.[27]

Throughout the years from 1650 to 1658, however, the strong hand in the family continued to be that of Grandfather George Etherege, who undertook—in his own words—to support "the needy and fatherless children" of George and Mary "as in nature and conscience he thought he was bound to do." Not long after Captain Etherege's death, Richard Powney paid his daughter the remaining two hundred pounds due according to the marriage arrangement, and her brother-in-law John Whitfield urged Grandfather Etherege to complete his bargain with Powney to provide an estate for the children worth sixty-six pounds a year. Although he was then seventy-three, Etherege delayed his decision, refusing even to tell Powney what his assets were. But a serious illness in the spring of 1654 forced him to face the facts of his depleted resources and the family's considerable needs and led to a number of family conferences, confrontations, and bitter exchanges over the disposition of his estate.

A Disputed Inheritance

The events that precipitated John Etherege's lawsuit against his father and his nephew George, the future playwright, have been alluded to already, but the importance of the outcome of that suit to the formation of young George's attitudes and to his financial situation requires an outline of the main events, as best they can be deduced from sometimes conflicting testimony.

When Grandfather George Etherege purchased property in Kent in 1628, he inserted the names of his two sons George and John on the deed in order to protect himself against encumbrances on the land. At the same time, however, a legacy came to him from his brother-in-law Rixman's will requiring a payment of fifty pounds to each of the three Etherege children. Since the eldest was abroad and the others were in their teens, Etherege understandably withheld any payment and—as the years passed—he wrote off the legacies as money expended on the children's education.

At the time of his illness in the spring of 1654, when it appeared that the old man might not recover, members of his family—Mary, her younger brother John Powney, Christopher Newstead, old Powney, and Powney's son-in-law John Whitfield—began discussing with him the disposition of his estate, pressing him to make provision for the younger children of Captain George, and he promised them he would soon do so. Shortly after that, it appears, Grace Luckins urged her master to remember his son John and more numerous family and was told that the Kent lands were in John's name and that of his dead brother Captain George. She immediately informed John and he confirmed the fact by sending to the Rolls and consulting the deed. When he confronted his father with the knowledge and threatened to take possession of the land, the old man—too ill and tired to quarrel—told him to draw up a will in his own favor, promising to leave the property to him at his death if he, Grandfather George, could retain it undisturbed for the rest of his life. This was done and for a time matters appeared to be settled, with both sides—John on the one and his nephew George and friends on the other—thinking they had the advantage.

In the meantime, then, before his stratagem was discovered,

Grandfather Etherege set about placing Captain George's children. No reference to the place found for Anne, the eldest, appears in the material uncovered by Foster,[28] nor to the placing of the two youngest children; but fifty pounds was given in 1654 to Mr. George Gosnold, attorney of Beaconsfield, Buckinghamshire, to take the young George Etherege as clerk,[29] and a smaller amount was given the following year to apprentice John to a surgeon bound for the East Indies. John is not heard of again, and it is clear that by the time of the trial he was dead. In 1656, with the lawsuit against him pending or already underway, Grandfather Etherege placed Margaret with a sempster in the New Exchange at a cost of twenty-five pounds.

The lawsuit had its immediate beginning about September 1655 when the two divines, Christopher Newstead and John Etherege, met in London and each learned for the first time of Grandfather George Etherege's deception. When John showed the will he had extracted from his father during his illness, Newstead, who understood the younger George and other grandchildren to be the intended heirs, told John that "it did not saviour [*sic*] of religion or become a Divine . . . to endeavor to gett away all his ffather's estate from his eldest brother's Children." Shortly after this angry meeting, John charged Grandfather Etherege, in the presence of Newstead and Thomas Cherry, with tricking him, and the old man admitted that he had allowed John to make out the will, knowing he could revoke it when he wished, and he rebuked the younger son for his undutiful conduct. John replied—according to Newstead's testimony—that his father would do nothing for the seven children of a godly man (John) but he "did not care how much hee did for ye seed of ye wicked ye Children of a Rebell" (i.e., of Captain Etherege). But John's pleading and storming were to no avail; his father continued to hold the deeds and refused to honor his earlier promise to John to will him the Kent properties.

While it is tempting to see the divine of Tangmer (Uncle John) as the villain in all of this bitterness, the rascal who would break his old father's heart and steal away our hero's estate, it must be admitted that John had reason to be suspicious that a plot lay behind the father's apparent change of heart. John's own family was large, after all, and its needs were great; and however much he may have taken advantage of his father's illness in extracting the will, John had reason to believe that the family and friends of the younger George were using their numbers and proximity to the old man to take an even greater advantage. And so John followed the simplest course open to him: he traveled over to the farms of Hollenden and Oldwood in Kent at Christmas time, 1655, and forced tenant Nicholas Reader to pay all rents to him.

The response of Grandfather Etherege to this development was prompt: on 10 January he signed an indenture conveying the Kent property to the children of his son Captain George, but retaining it for his own use during his lifetime. Monday the tenth was a market day in Maidenhead and Grandfather Etherege had to go twice to beg his brother-in-law Thomas Cherry to leave his fabric shop and come to witness the signing at the Greyhound Inn (where King Charles I had earlier bidden farewell to his chidren and where Milton's Quaker acquaintance Thomas Ellwood was to be arrested on a Sunday five years later).[30] Cherry reported the old man's anger at his son John, "a Vile man" who attempted to force a favorable will, and his pleasure at thus fulfilling the 1634 marriage agreement: "When hee had sealed ye same Indenture (said Cherry) . . . seemed to bee very ioyfull and glad and did say hee was very glad and well sattisfied that itt was done."

The tactic, however, did not succeed; John gathered confederates and continued to collect the rent from Nicholas Reader. In May the elder Etherege drew up a second indenture, this time conveying the property to Whitfield and John Powney (young George's "nere friend and guardian") to hold in trust, and John Etherege was sent for to sign the transfer. Of course, he refused and immediately instituted a suit against his father, the trustees, and young George, charging an attempt to defraud him of lands purchased with his money and settled on him. At this point, then, begins the year-long series of lawsuits, so strangely overlooked by many students of Etherege (even after Foster's publication of their essentials) but very useful to an understanding of the relationship between Sir George's early life and his dramatic compositions.

By April of the following year the skein of charge and countercharge was so tangled that a commission of the Court of Chancery began the first of several hearings, calling in witnesses to the ancient Bull Inn, presenting interrogatories and taking depositions. John was there, of course, with only Grace Luckins to take his side, and as one of the plantiffs young George must have been there, among the Powneys, Ethereges, and others who came to depose on his and Grandfather Etherege's behalf. In June the hearings ended, and on 10

December 1657, Judge Chaloner Chute handed down his decision. It was remarkably evenhanded, as balanced as the career of Chute himself, defense counsel for Archbishop Laud in 1644 and Speaker of the House of Commons in 1659. Chute ordered that Grandfather Etherege pay one hundred pounds to his son John and will another one hundred pounds to him, with the land as security. On receipt of the first amount John was, in his turn, to convey the premises to the younger George Etherege and the other heirs, according to the terms of the 10 January indenture. Although the elder Etherege had laid out a very large amount on John's education, reasoned Chute, he had not accounted for the fifty pounds willed to his son many years before, nor could John's many children be forgotten for they "are alsoe the grandchildren of the said George Etherege and unprovided for."

John made abortive attempts to oppose Judge Chute's decision, continuing into 1659, because upon the death of Grandfather Etherege in March or April 1658,[31] young George became heir to the Kent lands, worth forty pounds a year, and perhaps inherited a share of his grandfather's other property as well.[32] The elder Etherege's will has not been discovered, but Newstead testified that the future playwright was the chief heir, "Charged with the payment of severall Legacyes to the younger Children." The ninety-eight-acre estate in the Bermuda Islands was sold about this time,[33] and the remaining interest in the Manor of Ives disposed of, and some or all of that money might well have gone to the children of Captain Etherege.

The income from the Kent properties, thirty-six pounds a year after taxes, was by no means a great fortune, but it would have been quite enough to maintain an unmarried young gentleman like George Etherege in comfort, if not in style,[34] had he not been obligated by terms of his grandfather's will to share a portion of it with the younger children—presumably Richard and Elizabeth—at the same time that he continued to have legal expenses in connection with his uncle's resistance to Chute's decision. The placing of the two children would have been a concern for young George from 1658 into 1659, as would his uncle's continued efforts to contest the Chute decision. As late as 21 June 1659, for example, George and his solicitors were back in Chancery to hear a judgment requiring John to give his nephew a bond of one hundred fifty pounds for failure to fulfill the court's requirements. The suit was finally settled in George's favor on 14 July 1659.[35] Thus it was that the two great events of his young adulthood came about at nearly the same time—his freedom to enjoy his estate and the Restoration of the monarchy.

While the troublesome litigation over the Kent properties ended thus in his favor, the experience can be considered a capstone to the long series of events that had burdened young George's spirit from boyhood on: first the separation from his father in about 1642, then the climate of opinion in Maidenhead, where nearly everybody hated purveyors and where Puritanism was strong enough to make Captain Etherege's association with a Catholic queen the source of considerable embarrassment. Then there had been the turbulent events of the Civil War, with Roundhead regiments mustering in Maidenhead Thicket, troops quartered everywhere in the village, and the bridge across the nearby Thames River broken down again and again to prevent the king's cavalry from crossing.[36] Next in rapid succession had come the execution of Charles, the death in France of Captain Etherege, and the marriage of Mary to Chaplain Newstead. Apprenticed at eighteen, young Etherege had had held out to him by his grandfather the expectation of a modest estate, only to have those hopes jeopardized in a long lawsuit—brought by his uncle John, a divine—that led in the end to the grandfather's death.

Like Jonathan Swift, who had never known his father and whose Royalist grandfather had been ruined by the Civil War, Etherege must have felt a deep sense of loss at his father's exile and early death, and that feeling was intensified into hatred in later years by the knowledge that he had been disinherited by the Rebellion and the Puritan interregnum and very nearly deprived of the little that was his by the machinations of his uncle John, whose sympathies were enthusiastically with the Roundhead cause. No wonder the plays contain hits against Oliver Cromwell, as the patron of knaves and traitors (*The Comical Revenge,* 1.1); against the clergy, as self-serving tricksters (*She Would If She Could,* 1.1); and even some otherwise gratuitous ridicule of the "Gentlemen of the long Robe" (judges) in *The Man of Mode,* 1.1). In twenty-three years of life young George Etherege had been well equipped by circumstances, and perhaps by nature as well, to be a fit companion for the cynical and indolent younger gentlemen and aristocrats that were soon to gather in London about a cynical and indolent sovereign, a generation whose family life and education had been disrupted by war, exile, and confiscation, and whose moral principles had been developed against a background of religious intolerance and broken agreements for which Cavaliers and Puritans were equally responsible.

If there was any stability left in such a chaotic world, in Etherege's estimation, it was to be found in the two social institutions of family and fellowship, the only verities that survive the general laughter at human nature and institutions in the three comedies that were shortly to begin coming from his pen. In the first of these in particular, *The Comical Revenge,* performed in 1664 but set in the mid-1650s, Etherege may well have created the Lord Bevill family as an idealization of his own, with his grandfather as the magnanimous Bevill, his exiled father providing a model for the wrongly imprisoned Bruce, whose "honor was fed with vast expense of blood," and others from the home circle at Maidenhead fleshing out the characters of the heroic plot. He constructed in all three plays, certainly, a dramatic world that affirmed both the validity of marriage and family and the superiority of the upper class.

In their conclusions the plays give to women the all-important prize in the contest between the sexes. They are the victors over the institution of fellowship, and they are the civilizers of society and perpetuators of the species. Moreover, the plays express with confidence the rightness of the restored Cavaliers, affirming the "Virtues that in Courts are taught" (*The Comical Revenge,* 3.6) and offering reassurance to a generation of Royalists who had felt themselves inferior in breeding to their more polished hosts across the channel and who had become suspicious of the worth of their own culture in the face of catastrophic defeats at home at the hands of fanatics and parliamentarians.

Law Student

From the time of his apprenticeship in 1654 until at least August 1658,[37] young George Etherege was in the service of attorney George Gosnold of Beaconsfield, Buckinghamshire, laboring at the various chores that must occupy the time of every solicitor's clerk. But life there could hardly have been dull for a young man of intelligence and spirit and—perhaps—literary aspirations. It may even be that the young Etherege met Edmund Waller there. The controversial poet, who lived on the nearby estate of Hall Barn, was well known for his Royalist sympathies, but he had also been a law student at Lincoln's Inn and so he would have held an additional interest for Etherege. All that is certain, however, is that Etherege admired Waller's verse, gave Dorimant several passages to quote in *The Man of Mode* many years later, and lamented Waller's death in 1687.

The position as Gosnold's apprentice must have had its own appeal to Etherege's active mind. If ever there was the promise of an exciting career, it was the law in 1654, in the middle of an intense debate across England on the nature, function, and extent of government. In the preceding year, for instance, Cromwell's Barebones Parliament had established a committee to institute legal reforms, and lawyers were sent rushing to the defense of English common law. The years that followed saw no letup in political ferment, with new constitutions being written and rewritten with remarkable frequency and new parliaments forming on new principles almost as often. The position with Gosnold also gave Etherege a chance to travel, perhaps requiring him to stay away for many days at a time on business, as seems to have been the case in June 1656 when Uncle John Etherege's bill of complaint was presented to George in London by the Sheriff of Middlesex.[38]

Moreover, it was with Gosnold's influence that Etherege was admitted to study law at Clement's Inn in London in early 1659. How long he was there is not known, but there and under Gosnold he learned the law well, as can be seen in the many letters he wrote in the 1680s, some of them, like the letter to Middleton of 14 March 1686, close analyses of questions of inheritance and property law, and others, like those to Carlingford and d'Albeville in the waning months of his residency, shrewd discussions of the complex legal issues between James II and Prince William of Orange. One letter, in fact, written to Viscount Preston in late 1688, is a veritable short lecture on the laws and institutions of England, their division into common law and statute law, and the prerogatives of the king and the privileges of his subjects.

Etherege's formal education in law began on 19 February 1659 when he was admitted to Clement's Inn, one of the eight Inns of Chancery, where young gentlemen prepared themselves for advanced study at one of the Inns of Court or perhaps simply learned enough law to manage their own business affairs.[39] His term of service to Gosnold was up at about that time, for according to a rule of the Judges of the Upper Bench in 1654 the term of lawyers' apprentices was to last for five years; the same rule required that he pass an examination before he could qualify as an attorney.[40] Enrollment at Clement's Inn would have given the finishing touches to his training under Gosnold and would have enabled him better to pass his exam.

As Frederick Bracher discovered in his investigation of Etherege's stay at Clement's, the future playwright could have had a very thorough legal education there, especially in the practice of common law, as well as training in Law-Latin and Law-French. He would also have had the opportunity to learn such social skills as singing, dancing, and fencing, and to attend musical and dramatic performances at an academy maintained by the Inns of Chancery. There would have been lectures by barristers from the Inns of Court, and in the evenings exercises in which three students would argue points of law in imaginary cases. From time to time Etherege would have gone to observe trials at one of the nearby courts, and he would have continued to assist Gosnold with legal work, for the eminent attorney was a senior member at Clement's Inn and became principal there in 1670.

Along with young George Etherege, whose home was recorded as "Beconsfeild in the County of Buckingham," were a number of other young men like John Hunt, Richard Middlemore, Francis Johnson, and John Giles, who had also been enrolled early in 1659 by Principal John Grene to begin their formal study of the law. What sort of life would they have led after study hours and on holidays? Some idea of what they should not have done, says Bracher, can be gotten from the *Pension Book of Clement's Inn.* Listed there are such misdemeanors as taking food without permission, fighting with fists or with weapons, going to a tavern for any business but honest eating and drinking, lying with a woman in the Inn or the parish, and throwing water and emptying chamber pots out of the windows. Naturally, there were fines for anybody who might be caught.

A great many dramatic entertainments also were available to the young students at Clement's, both at the academy associated with the Inns of Chancery and in the neighborhood, and Etherege must have been frequently in one of these audiences. Between 1657 and 1660, for example, he could have seen *The Countryman, or Clown,* a farce that was often performed at the nearby Inns of Court.[41] He might have seen as well a number of private—and illegal—performances at Gibbons's Tennis Court nearby, at the Salisbury Court Theatre, Rutland House, the Red Bull, and the Cockpit—all within a few blocks of Clement's Inn. Very likely his appetite for good theater was whetted by these fleeting and surreptitious dramatic performances from 1656, when he visited London, through 1659, when he was steadily there. From 1660 until the performance of his first play in 1664, whether he continued his studies at all or was simply a gentleman of leisure, he would have been a frequent theatergoer, especially after plays became legal again, for he knew his stagecraft well when he himself came to write.

In view of Etherege's knowledge of the law, it is not surprising that one of the early legacies of his clerkship with Gosnold and his studies in London should have been the scattering of legal terminology that one finds throughout his comedies. Many of these reflect more than a mere layman's knowledge of the world of law: in *She Would If She Could* there is Sir Oliver's use of terms like "cause" and "premunire" in favor of their less technical synonyms, Courtall's appeal to Gazette as his "faithful counsellor," and other figurative references to jury bribing, sealing before a witness, arrests upon execution, reprieves, forfeits, mortgages, and the like. There is in *The Man of Mode* Medley's famous characterization of Dorimant as a man of great employment, with "more mistresses now depending than the most eminent lawyer in England has causes" (2.1),[42] and his malicious observation to Lady Townley that "Young men who are brought up under practising lawyers prove the abler counsel when they come to be called to the bar themselves" (3.2).

More important than these occasional and largely figurative uses of legal language in the dramatic works, however, is Etherege's structural use of situations that involve issues of law. Three of the four plots in *The Comical Revenge* turn on questions of legality: whether Graciana is bound to Bruce or to Beaufort, what the outcome will be of Wheadle's scheme (riddled with legal "devices") to defraud Sir Nicholas Cully, and whether lawful marriage will result from the mutual pursuit of Sir Frederick and the Widow Rich. And Etherege underscores the legal ancestry of his first play with two of three epilogues, the first the widow's comic announcement that she has tricked Sir Frederick by making the gentlemen of the audience the trustees of her wealth, and the third—spoken perhaps by Sir Frederick—a reminder to the audience that they are the jury and the author is the prisoner, and, until they have filled the house once or twice more, he cannot be sure what his sentence will be.

Although the later two plays show somewhat fewer traces of the influence of Etherege's legal career, the issue of lawful marriage continues as the central concern in both, with the two sets of gay couples in *She Would If She Could* involved throughout the play in negotiations that end in a double engagement, and with Dorimant and Harriet in *The Man of Mode* threatening to resolve at last the question of whether the rake-hero will continue his libertine ways or will be confined in legal wedlock. While there is only a scattering of allusions to the law in the later two comedies, three of them are reminiscent of what we know of events in Etherege's own life. Besides the remark by Medley, already mentioned, referring to clerks "brought up under practising lawyers," there is Rakehell's offhand observation to Sir Joslin to remind us of Uncle John Etherege's situation in the 1657 suit: "you know a younger brother [John?] has not wherewithal to rebate the edge of a witness and mollify the hearts of a jury" (4.2). The central device of the forged letters in the long amatory duel between the two couples in *She Would If She Could* brings to mind, of course, the 1657 lawsuit against young George. While signatures and handwriting would have been crucial in nearly all the legal work Etherege did for Gosnold, the will forged by Uncle John and his mother Mary's identification of the handwriting in letters by him and by her late husband were crucial pieces of evidence in the dispute over the lands willed to young George by his grandfather.

Beyond these suggestions that in some of the situations and in the language of the comedies George Etherege drew upon his legal experiences, there is the certainty that in a larger sense his apprenticeship as a writer was served under Gosnold and at Clement's Inn and that the intense exposure he must have had to a variety of persons and legal entanglements helped sharpen the sense of character and of situation that every playwright must possess. Most of the best comic playwrights of the Restoration, interestingly enough, had legal training or careers in law before they wrote for the stage, including William Wycherley, Thomas Shadwell, Thomas Southerne, and William Congreve. And while legal experience is obviously not a prerequisite for writing comedy, an important part of the attorney's work must be the sorting out of the truth from a number of contradictory sources, the kind of experience that would be a valuable prelude to the constructing of plots. Etherege shows his skill in plot-making throughout the three plays, but nowhere to such a good effect as in his middle comedy, *She Would If She Could,* especially the denouement of act 5, where Courtall and Lady Cockwood "explain" all the points of the plot to the satisfaction of the rest of the company—and to the delight of the audience, who are aware of how completely the truth has been altered to fit the requirements of the moment.

What little we know of Etherege's career in law really comes to this, then, that he served as clerk for several years to a prominent Beaconsfield attorney and studied for a while at one of the Inns of Chancery, and that his plays and letters are evidence that he knew his craft well and continued his interest in matters of law and government throughout his life. Immediately after the time of his apprenticeship with Gosnold we have only two hints of his activities and whereabouts, as I have already noted: on 19 February 1659 he was admitted to Clement's Inn and on 21 June 1659 he was in London with his solicitors to hear an order by William Glascocke, directing Uncle John Etherege to give a bond to secure the Kent property from his wife's claim of dower.[43] Beyond this evidence in support of Oldys's statement that for a time George studied the municipal laws at one of the Inns of Court in London, there is virtually no information about Etherege for the next five years. His proficient use of French in the plays and his apparent knowledge of some of Molière's comedies suggest strongly, however, that he was in Paris sometime between mid–1659 and the 1663–64 theatrical season when he readied *The Comical Revenge; or, Love in a Tub,* for production at the Duke's Playhouse in Lincoln's Inn Fields.[44]

"Playing the Fool in Verse and Prose"

What motives could impel a young man about town in 1662 or 1663 to try his hand at the writing of a comedy? Etherege had strong feelings to express about his family and their suffering, of course, because of the Civil War and the Puritans. He had accumulated a storehouse of impressions at Beaconsfield, Maidenhead, and London and at whatever other ports he had touched in his young life, chiefly impressions of people whom he might turn into comic characters, and certainly he had a vision of the new kind of dramatic realism that would lead him to people the stage with personages who might have stepped out of the very audiences who crowded the pit, boxes, and gallery of Davenant's converted tennis-court theater, where his first play would be performed. The new age, furthermore, that had been ushered in by the return of the king, Charles II, had already seen a blossoming of the literary arts, and George had recently tried his wings in poetry at least once, turning out an imitative set of bawdy comic verses called "The Imperfect Enjoyment," which was now circulating in manuscript copies.[45]

Perhaps the catalyst that led Etherege to play the fool in verse and prose, as he termed it, was the death of his stepfather Christopher Newstead in 1662, when, according to one account his wife Mary Newstead "was reduced to great want . . . and was supported by the charity of the Corporation for Ministers' Widows."[46] The *Dictionary of National Biography* account, however, seems inaccurate or exaggerated inasmuch as Mary was in reality left with adequate means of support. The will of her husband, recently discovered in the Public Record Office,[47] contains this item: "I give unto my loving wife all that which by the Articles upon our Marriage were sealed by her ffriends and my selfe. And I charge my sonnes aforesaid to be loveing and respectfull to her." The two sons were Christopher and Fullhurst, to both of whom Newstead left the household furniture and some property in Lincolnshire. The friends of Mary would likely have included her father Richard, her brothers, and perhaps her brother-in-law William Canning; and the context of the will clearly suggests that the "all" of the marriage articles would have been adequate to sustain Widow Newstead in comfort. It now seems likely, consequently, that it was George Etherege's desire to improve his own as well as his mother's financial circumstances that finally brought him to write his first play and to submit it to Sir William Davenant, for the slight inheritance from his grandfather could not have supported a truly gentlemanly existence in London, and his position as eldest son demanded that he accept some responsibility for his mother's maintenance.

If Etherege had any reputation at all in London before the opening of *The Comical Revenge,* whether as law student, idler, gambler, or bawdy poet, on the morning after the premier he awoke—like Lord Byron nearly 150 years later—to find himself famous. The details of that first performance at the Duke's Playhouse, it is true, are not known, and even the exact date remains a mystery, although it was very likely in March 1664.[48] But the actors who performed it were some of the most popular ever to appear on the Restoration stage, and the production was the most successful comic piece in the history of Davenant's company, bringing it "more Reputation and Profit [as prompter John Downes said] than any preceding Comedy; the Company taking in a Months time at it 1000£."[49]

By the spring of 1664 Sir William Davenant's Company had been in business for over three years, producing at least forty or fifty different plays in that time, and so the triumphant production of Etherege's new comedy was an event of major significance in the life of the Lincoln's Inn Fields Playhouse and one more victory in the rivalry with the King's Company. It was an especially timely success too, for in January and February 1664 Davenant's lavish production of *Henry VIII* and a competing production by Thomas Killigrew's company of *The Indian Queen*—characterized by Evelyn as having "rich Scenes as the like had never ben seene here"[50]—had temporarily exhausted the audience's interest in stage spectacles and had made the new comedy a welcome diversion. The statement by Downes indicates that *The Comical Revenge* ran for a full month, and his remark that one thousand pounds was taken in during that time tends to support the idea that the play ran for as long as twenty to twenty-five nights: in so small a house as Davenant's the daily box-office take could scarcely have exceeded fifty pounds, except for the first night when prices probably were increased, and very likely it averaged closer to forty pounds.[51] If there had been that many consecutive performances, of course, Etherege's comedy would have had the longest recorded run of any play in London since the Restoration, and that fact would have given added luster to his success.[52]

The auditorium of the Duke's Playhouse, while its size severely limited box-office income, had the advantage of permitting a realistic and extremely intimate kind of theater, with the audience only a few feet from the stage. For a time after the Restoration, Davenant had tried out the old theaters in London, experimenting with scenery as one way of adding new life to the drama of the previous age. But his earlier successes in 1656 with opera at Gibbons's Tennis Court and his observation of tennis-court theaters in France led him in 1660 to choose Lisle's in the parish of St. Clement Danes[53] (a stone's throw from Etherege's law school, Clement's Inn) to remodel into a sumptuous new playhouse where the depth of the stage would permit experiments with scenic effects and where problems of lighting and acoustics would be minimized by the small size of the house. Pepys, for one, appreciated its qualities and criticized the slightly larger Hall theater in Whitehall (new in 1666) for the distance from the boxes to the stage.

While the exact measurements of the new Duke's House are not known, Professor Leslie Hotson has deduced from land transactions recorded in *The Black Book of Lincoln's Inn* that the structure was 75 feet long and 30 feet wide, as compared with 87 × 39½ feet at the Hall theater.[54] In her study of tennis-court theaters Elizabeth Scanlan proposes a measurement of 30 by 35 feet for the auditorium of the Duke's Playhouse, and she conjectures further that there were two levels of boxes around the hall with a single gallery above the front boxes and a pit extending from the front boxes to the stage, for a total capacity of 352 persons—an entirely reasonable calculation.[55]

Although the Restoration audience was largely of upper-class composition in the early years of the decade, it was nevertheless a varied lot,[56] as the pages of Pepys's *Diary* reveal. Whether the king and queen were in the audience at the first or subsequent performances of *The Comical Revenge* we do not know, but it was a common occurrence for the royal couple to attend and for the duke and duchess of York and a crowd of retainers to appear with them in the royal boxes. Besides the possible attendance of the court, there would have been representatives of the nobility and members of the professions, citizens, whores, gallants, and even shopkeepers, apprentices, and others from the lower classes. At a performance of Dryden's *Feign'd Innocence* at the Duke's in January 1668 Pepys reflected on the variety of spectators there and on the changes in the composition of the audiences over the years: "Here a mighty company of citizens, 'prentices, and others; and it makes me observe, that when I begun first to be able to bestow a play on myself, I do not remember that I saw so many by half of the ordinary 'prentices and mean people in the pit at 2*s*. 6*d*. a-piece as now; I going for several years no higher than the 12*d*. and then the 18*d*. places."

Diarist John Evelyn had attended *The Comical Revenge* during its opening run and had found it "facetious." When Samuel Pepys finally came to see the play—some ten months after its premiere—he thought it "very merry, but only so by gesture, not wit at all." And his subsequent viewing of two performances in 1666 and 1668 seems not to have changed his opinion. What he did like about Etherege's play was the acting, and particularly—one may surmise—the acting of the Bettertons. When the husband and wife were missing from the performance of the comedy at Whitehall, Pepys "had no manner of pleasure in the play," and the reception accorded *She Would If She Could* (1668), in which the Bettertons did not appear, helped to give it a blow from which it never recovered. The diarist overheard Etherege in the pit after that play, complaining bitterly to Buckhurst and Sedley that the actors were unprepared and that Henry Harris could not even sing a catch in it.

Despite his youth Thomas Betterton was already one of the acknowledged stars of the London stage. He had begun his acting career as a female impersonator, but after a short time his skill won him such varied lead roles as Faustus, Mercutio, Sir Toby Belch, and Hamlet. His special forte, however, was the heroic or tragic character, having been instructed, so it was said, by Davenant in the acting style favored by Shakespeare himself. Hence the part of Beaufort in Etherege's first play, while minor, was especially suited to his genius.

Pepys thought him "the best actor in the world." Playing opposite Betterton was his wife Mary Saunderson (also a favorite of Pepys), whose long succession of serious roles made her ideal for the part of the perplexed Graciana in *The Comical Revenge*. Mary Davis played her sweet-voiced sister Aurelia; and William Smith, Betterton's rival in heroic roles, portrayed the noble Bruce. Interestingly enough, these two actors were to continue their stage rivalry in 1676 in the best of Etherege's comedies, with Smith playing Sir Fopling to Betterton's Dorimant.

Fortunately for *The Comical Revenge,* the actors in the lower plots were among the most successful comedians of the London stage. Despite Etherege's criticism four years later, Henry Harris, who acted the lead role of Sir Frederick Frollick, was so popular with audiences, "the King and every body else crying him up so high,"[57] that in the summer of 1663 he had attempted to leave the Duke's and join the rival King's Company when Davenant refused to meet his salary demands. King Charles, however, would not permit the move, and shortly before Etherege's first play opened, he mollified Harris by appointing him Yeoman of the Revels.[58]

Samuel Sandford portrayed Wheadle, the confidence man who contrives the plot to bilk Cully. He is characterized by Antony Aston as "Round-shoulder'd, Meagre-fac'd, Spindle-shank'd, Splay-footed, with a sour Countenance, and long lean Arms," and was thought by King Charles to be "the best *Villain* in the World."[59] Wheadle's associate in crime, Palmer, was played by Cave Underhill, already famous as the First Grave-digger in *Hamlet* and considered by Davenant to be "the truest comedian in his Company."[60] Many years later Colley Cibber described him in his middle age as able to act "the most lumpish, moping Mortal, that ever made Beholders merry."[61]

The dupe on whom these two scoundrels work their confidence game is Sir Nicholas Cully, developed by James Nokes into the master role of his career, the very picture of "piteous Pusillanimity . . . and palpable Ignorance" (said Cibber).[62] The remaining three players who John Downes tells us had parts in the play were Henry Norris (Lovis), just beginning his career as a supporting actor; Joseph Price (Dufoy), described by Downes as "that Inimitable Sprightly Actor"; and Jane Long (Widow), who later gained renown in such "breeches parts" as Dulcino in James Shirley's *The Grateful Servant* and the justice in Betterton's *The Woman Made Justice*.

The realism of the characters and the setting of *The Comical Revenge* accorded well with the realistic style of comic acting in vogue during the Restoration period and certainly contributed to the play's success. There were, to be sure, enough asides in the comedy to weaken the illusion of reality, and the heroic upper plot was no doubt acted in that highly stylized manner that required a whole range of melodramatic gestures for the expression of a variety of emotions. In the three lower plots, however, the new realism of Etherege's comic style and of Restoration acting—much of it owing to the introduction of women on the stage[63]—combined to give Etherege an instant reputation for dramatic genius and to make *The Comical Revenge* one of the more influential comedies in the annals of the English theater.

The history of the performance of *The Comical Revenge* is spotty, to say the least. Although Gerard Langbaine reported that it was always well received, during Etherege's lifetime it was acted only ten more times that we know of and perhaps twice more in 1689 and 1690 when it was reprinted by Henry Herringman. By then Etherege had been away from England for four or five years—first at Ratisbon, where the mere mention of the theater in a letter from William Jephson made Sir George (as he wrote in reply in August 1688) "impatient to see the scene of my past Triumphs and Loves"—and then at Paris, where he had gone in hopes of serving the exiled King James. Performed once in December 1695 and reprinted in 1697, *The Comical Revenge* was revived at least two more times before the century closed. Throughout the first two decades of the eighteenth century it continued to be played, with some twenty recorded productions during that time. In later years, however, it appeared on stage only infrequently (three times from 1720 to 1729), and in the nineteenth and twentieth centuries was virtually forgotten, a fate that awaited both of Etherege's later comedies as well.

"O Thou Immortall Source of Idleness" (Dryden)

The immediate effects of the success of *The Comical Revenge* were to bring young George Etherege the author's share of the third night's receipts and—more important—to launch him on the career for which he was to become famous as "Easy Etherege" and "Gentle George," the wit, idler, and friend of that growing circle of wild young gentlemen who were familiars of the king and his brother, the duke of York. Among the earliest of Etherege's acquaintance was the young Lord Buckhurst, to be created earl of Dorset in 1677, and destined to be George's lifelong friend and a patron of poets, the Maecenas of the Restoration. How soon the two men came to know each other is not certain, but the twenty-year-old Buckhurst had in June 1663 attained his first notoriety in London because of the infamous Cock Tavern escapade,[64] and Etherege quite possibly entered his circle not long after. It may be that event and other adventures of the young wits of Buckhurst's acquaintance that provided the fledgling playwright with a real-life model for Sir Frederick Frollick and his drunken, window-breaking, brawling career in *The Comical Revenge*. Ripples from the Cock Tavern adventure had spread rapidly, and several accounts of the event there have come down to us, including a frank and detailed one by the ubiquitous Pepys.[65]

In outline the story is simple enough: Lord Buckhurst, Sir Charles Sedley, and Sir Thomas Ogle—having laced their dinner with too much wine—proceeded to scandalize the neighborhood by stripping off their clothes, exhibiting themselves, and hurling insults and empty bottles from the balcony of the tavern into the street below. A fight followed when a mob stormed the tavern door, and, according to Anthony à Wood, the three nearly lost their lives. Sedley was arrested and fined two thousand marks, and Buckhurst was chastised by the judge. Such conduct, while obviously not condoned, was recognized as characteristic of high-spirited young gentlemen, and Sir Frederick Frollick would have been entirely at home in their company. Of course, Etherege himself, we know, later took part in a number of scandalous escapades, both in London and (incredibly) in Ratisbon, where his conduct was doubly shocking to the staid Germans because he was the king's representative and was past fifty to boot.

Not long after the Cock Tavern event, it appears, Etherege and Buckhurst became acquainted, perhaps when Buckhurst took an interest in the play Etherege was writing, for Etherege tells us in the dedication to Buckhurst of *The Comical Revenge* that the writing of the comedy "was a means to make me known to your Lordship." By the winter of 1663–64 the two were engaged in an exchange of obscene verse epistles regarding their amatory escapades,[66] and by the summer of 1664, when *The Comical Revenge* was licensed for the press and, presumably, printed, Etherege announced himself as "long since dedicated" to Buckhurst. He was dedicated as well, no doubt, to that growing circle of wits in which Sedley and Buckingham were leading lights, the circle of wits that was helping make the court of Charles

II at once the most brilliant and the most debauched in the island's history.

If, in Pepysian fashion, George Etherege had taken stock of himself in the spring of 1664, on the eve of his entrance into a strikingly new course of life, he would have been gratified at the meteoric rise of his fortunes. At twenty-eight he was the toast of London and a member of the wittiest and most reckless band of young gentlemen ever to haunt Westminster and the City. In his appearance and manners, furthermore, he would have seemed the very epitome of Castiglione's ideal courtier—of moderate build, accomplished in poetry, and skilled in every grace of conversation and polite conduct. Although no portrait exists, there is one description of his physical appearance at this time and many anecdotes to illustrate his character. The actor John Bowman told William Oldys many years later that the young Etherege was a "fair, slender, genteel man," "very affable and courteous, of a sprightly and generous temper." He loved companionship, as we know from his letters and the anecdotes about him, and delighted in conversation, becoming legendary early in his lifetime as Gentle George and Easy Etherege. The Homeric epithets rest as easily on his shoulders as do those of "Manly" Wycherley and "Brother" Van on his fellow playwrights', and the terms capture the essence of his personal charm, a negligence in manner and a generosity of spirit that made him among the most sought-after of the wits who frequented the Bear, the Rose, and the Dog and Partridge.

One story about him, told by his fellow poet Thomas Otway, is from a later period in Etherege's life, but from what we know of his conduct early and late, it is probably typical of his genius for smoothing the occasionally troubled waters of good fellowship. While Etherege was dining at Locket's Ordinary (said Otway), some company there, "who were highly incensed at some ill management of their entertainment or attendance, were all in violent passion with the waiters, so that Mrs. Locket came up; when Sir George told her they were so provoked that he could find in his heart to pull the nosegay out of her bosom and throw the flowers in her face, which turned all their rage to a jest."[67] On another occasion, when his debt at Locket's had become burdensome and he began to stay away, Mrs. Locket sent a messenger to his lodging, demanding the money. His reply was witty: if she took any further steps (he wrote), he would come and ______ her. When the outraged Mrs. Locket prepared to go to Etherege's lodging, however, her good-natured and equally witty husband Abraham commented: "Don't be so rash; there's no telling to what lengths a man will go when blinded by anger."[68]

Etherege cultivated a reputation for laziness to the end of his days and was chided for it by his friends almost from the very beginning. The long hiatus between *She Would If She Could* and *The Man of Mode* was singled out by an anonymous poet as particular evidence of his sloth:

> But Apollo had got gentle George in his eye,
> And frankly confest, of all men that writ,
> There's none had more fancy, sense, judgment and wit.
> But i' th' crying sin, idleness, he was so hardened,
> That his long seven years' silence was not to be pardoned.[69]

So jealous, in fact, was he of his reputation as London's idler sans peer that in later years he scolded Dryden in a letter for laying claim even to a small piece of the Kingdom of Sloth. Dryden, after invoking his correspondent as "thou immortall source of Idlenss," had gone on to claim kinship to Etherege and to cite examples of his own lethargy (letter of 16 February 1687). Etherege would have none of it, however, and in a mock tirade against Dryden's presumption he praised his friend's creative spirit and reasserted his own reputation as a complete idler: "Is it not enough that you excell in soe many eminent vertues, but you must be putting in for a vice which all the world knows is properly my Province. . . . I (whose every action of my life is a witness of my Idlenesse) little thought that you, who have rais'd so many Immortall monuments of your Industrie, durst have set up to be my Rival . . ." (*Letters,* 102–3). Many of the other personal letters that Etherege wrote to friends carry reminders of the premium he placed upon his reputation for idleness. To his old gambling companion Lord Dover he wrote: "The life I have lead [*sic*] has afforded me little time to turn over bookes, but I have had leisure sufficient while I idly rowl'd about the Town to look into my self and know when I am too highly valu'd" (*Letters,* 166).

Although his choice of a career of pleasant leisure had come after a long apprenticeship in unhappiness and hard work, Etherege liked to claim that he had been intended by nature for an idle fellow and had been given "passions and qualities fitt for that blessed calling" (*Letters,* 185). He was no Rochester, certainly, who was introduced by his college tutor to the joys of debauchery at the tender age of fourteen, mastering their refinements before attaining his majority. Nevertheless, Etherege was able to throw himself wholeheartedly into the pleasures of London by the time he was twenty-eight, when his grandfather's estate had freed him from the law and his new friendship with Buckhurst had raised his sinning to a higher social level than before. By the time the two had met, Etherege could already boast of a long career as a whoremaster, bearing "the many scars Which he has gotten in those wars" ("Mr. Etherege's Answer," *Poems,* 43–45). The later correspondence, too, is shot full of references to the joys of sex as well as its occasional pains (including a reminder to Dryden that the two had once been rivals for the favors of the same woman), and the letters of Etherege's vengeful secretary Hugo Hughes describe Etherege's amatory debaucheries in Ratisbon with such detail that—even allowing a discount for malice—they rival the most sensational accounts that have come down to us about some of Etherege's London companions. The tales of Lord Buckhurst's and Sir Charles Sedley's "acting all the postures of lust and buggery" on the balcony of the Cock Tavern in 1663 or of Lord Rochester's "beastly prank" of running nude through Woodstock Park in 1677 were at least matched by Hughes's acounts of Etherege and two sisters dancing stark naked in his chambers, of Sir George and an Austrian friend running about the streets of Ratisbon "having nothing on but their shirts," and of his scandalous pursuit of the comedienne from Nurenberg. While we know little enough of Etherege's amorous amusements in the 1660s, we know a great deal about them in the 1680s, and his frequent confessions in the letters of his love of "the rustling of petticoats" indicates that the pursuit of sex so frankly admitted in the two verse epistles to Buckhurst in 1663 was lifelong and wholehearted.

Of his other love, gambling, there is little concrete evidence, beyond the references in *The Comical Revenge,* to its important part in his early life in London, before the 1670s when the rage for bassett and other games of chance swept London. Nevertheless, his later comments in the letters at least hint that his passion for play was of long standing, perhaps going back to the period immediately after the opening of *The Comical Revenge*. By 1685 and his appointment as King James's resident in Ratisbon, however, he was eager to escape London, very likely because of a combination of gambling debts and a troublesome wife. Although he indulged his passion long enough in Holland to win two hundred pounds and long enough in Ratisbon to lose it again, he vowed to avoid deep play thereafter and refrained from all but sixpenny ombre throughout the rest of his stay in Germany. Of his life as a gambler in London over many years he wrote to the earl of Dover, "I have preferr'd my pleasure to my profit and have followed what was likelier to ruin a fortune already made than make one: play and women" (14 June 1688).

The most forceful statement, however, of his former complete subjection to the lure of play in the London gaming houses comes in a letter to fellow gambler Robert Corbet, a brilliant description that might have appeared in one of the *Characters* by Sir Thomas Overbury or in a sketch by John Earle: a Gamester, writes Etherege, "is never well but when he is tugging at the Oar. If he happens to be at liberty, he runs about the Town impatient to find a Gally where he may put on his Chaine again." Besides skipping meals and neglecting his mistress, Sir George continues, the gambler avoids his friends, "and sometimes if they catch him and press him to go with them, tho' he hates a lye in his nature, he cannot forbear making a false excuse to get from them, being asham'd to own the Truth." And Etherege concludes, in a tone of deep remorse, "Neither Love nor envy can tear the minde with sharper passions than the variety of fortune plagues him with. I cou'd say a Thousand things more on this subject, but this is enough to lett you see I am yet sensible of the pangs I have suffer'd" (13 May 1688).

Gambler, then, and lover of women, Easy Etherege was fit company for the likes of Buckhurst, Sedley, Buckingham, and the precocious earl of Rochester. If he was never, like Rochester, drunk for five years together, at least he imbibed enough in his youth, by Oldys's report, to "spoil" his face. At Ratisbon, however, he plied the bottle with as much caution as Alexander Pope, and a verse letter from Dryden in 1686 indicates what Etherege's reputation in London had been in that regard: "For wine, to leave a whore or play / Was ne're your Excellencies way." It is likely, as a matter of fact, that Etherege in middle age was constitutionally unable to imbibe heartily, for he wrote to Buckingham that the German love of heavy drinking did not agree with "one of my Complexion" and that it would be a "great Constraint upon my Nature to sit out a Night's Entertainment with them . . ." (*Letters,* 68). A man need not be guilty of every excess, after all, to qualify as a rake.

Of the requirements for the high post of court wit in the 1660s and 1670s, Etherege had nearly all: he was poet and playwright, a lover of good fellowship, a ladies' man, a gamester, and enough of a wine-bibber to contrive to hold his own in the company that frequented Lockets or the Rose. Beyond these, however, he seems to have possessed to a high degree two attributes indispensable to a Restoration wit—personal vanity that approached foppishness and a code of honor that brooked no insult to himself or to his sovereign. The two characteristics are related, both branches growing from the same trunk of pride in his position as leading playwright, member of the gentry, and friend of dukes and earls. Of his vanity there is, perhaps, less evidence. Like Dorimant, no doubt, he liked to consider himself to be dressed always à la mode, just short of the excesses of Sir Fopling and his ilk, as in this exchange between Dorimant and his man Handy:

> DORIMANT: Leave your unnecessary fiddling; a wasp that's buzzing about a man's nose at dinner, is not more troublesome than thou art.
>
> HANDY: You love to have your clothes hang just, sir.
>
> DORIMANT: I love to be well dressed sir: and think it no scandal to my understanding.
>
> . . .
>
> That a man's excellency should lie in neatly tying of a ribbond, or a cravat! how careful's nature in furnishing the world with necessary coxcombs! (1.1)

But like Harriet, who found Dorimant "very courtly, and much affected," there were those among Etherege's acquaintance—among them Dean Lockier and Hugo Hughes—who thought him overdressed, in manners overrefined. Hughes charged that he was scorned in Ratisbon for his "foppishness of dress" (*Letters,* 308), and Lockier said to Spence: "Sir George Etherege was as thorough a fop as ever I saw; he was exactly his own Sir Fopling Flutter. And yet he designed Dorimant . . . for his own picture."[70] Fortunately, a description of Etherege in full courtly regalia has come down to us, confirming Hughes's comment and Lockier's portrait, a depiction of him as he appeared in about 1680 at a drinking party in a Channel-row tavern attended as well by his old friends Thomas Shadwell, Elkanah Settle, and Lord Buckhurst (by then the earl of Dorset). After some lines describing Dorset ("A"), the anonymous poet goes on to outline the person of Etherege ("B"):

Next unto A. B. took his place,
Or Sir *Fopling,* if you please.
I mean that Famous Limner, who
So exactly his own Picture drew.
Bless me! how neat a Wigg he has!
What a rich Watch and Pocket-Glass!
What a gay Suit trim'd all about!
Made by a *French-man* without doubt.
His Ruffles and Cravat's all Lace,
Poynt a Venice he says it is.
To what advantage does he wear
His rings? How stuft with Stones they are?
One having this Inscription,
My Plow is all my Portion.[71]

The detail in the passage leaves no doubt that the author of the lines, perhaps Thomas Ward, had observed Etherege closely and expected readers who knew him to accept the description as an accurate one of the man who said: "I must confess I am a Fop in my heart; . . . I have been so us'd to affectation that without the help of the aer [*sic*] of the Court what is naturall cannot touch me" (*Letters,* 170).

Foppish he may have been and lazy and cynical, but Etherege wore his honor on his sleeve and would fight to protect it at the drop of an insult. Although not reputed to be quarrelsome by nature, he nevertheless managed to become involved in a number of violent squabbles that were reported in contemporary gossip, and he seems as well to have been known for his ill treatment of servants. The earliest evidence of his involvement in a quarrel is his duel with Edmund Ashton in September 1671, but two earlier hints suggest that Etherege shared with his fellow Cavaliers a readiness to employ his sword in honor's defense. A century ago Edmund Gosse proposed Sir Frederick Frollick of *The Comical Revenge* as a self-portrait of Etherege, and the notion is an intriguing one. Sir Frederick's adventures—especially his always being "at wars with the Women,"[72] his all-night debauches, and his part in the duel between Beaufort and Bruce—accord well with what we know of Etherege during the 1680s. And he would hardly have been less reckless in his thirties than in his fifties.

Equally intriguing, but even more problematical, is the possibility that Sir Charles Sedley created Ned Estridge in *The Mulberry Garden* in the image of his friend George Etherege.[73] Of special interest, beyond the similarity of names (Estridge—Etheridge, Etherege), is the fact that Sedley's fop in that play brings his sword to the rescue of old Forecast, announces himself ready to fight for his mistress's bracelet of hair, and is quick to challenge Wildish to a duel (although he is readily talked out of it). Other characteristics of Estridge and Etherege agree, including their love of drink and women, their witty conversation, and their foppish dress. And the likelihood that Sedley had Etherege in mind is increased in several other ways: Etherege's second play, *She Would If She Could,* and Sedley's *The Mulberry Garden* were composed and rehearsed at about the same time and were performed within three months of each other in 1668; Sedley's central character Wildish appears to be closely modeled after Etherege's Sir Frederick Frollick; both plays are set during the Puritan interregnum; and in both a widow is pursued by a character who can be identified as Etherege. Such a hypothesis, furthermore, would help to explain why Etherege put Sedley on stage in 1676 as Medley in *The Man of Mode:* he was simply returning a half-humorous compliment.

Besides the battle with Ashton, which John Muddyman described as "the furious combat of Ashton and Etheridg, which ended hapily in a fall on Ashton's part,"[74] there is, as further evidence of Etherege's sometime quarrelsomeness, the tragic carouse at Epsom Wells in June 1676 which began with tossing fiddlers and beating the constable and ended with one rioter dead and Etherege and his two other friends (Rochester and George Bridges) in full flight;[75] and a tavern squabble the next year between Etherege and Henry Bulkeley during which Fleetwood Shepherd was wounded as he attempted to part the two men.[76] There is that anonymous character sketch of Etherege in 1680, concluding:

> Here I must his Description end,
> For fear he should a Challenge send.
> Tho' he had better stay at home
> To Hector Foot-boy, or a Groom.[77]

And four remarkable letters by secretary Hugo Hughes in 1686 and 1687 describe Sir George's gambling quarrels in Ratisbon, his window breaking and street brawling, and his abuse of his servants. Even if they make Etherege appear to be an aging Pap Finn rather than the witty and easy author of three plays, Hughes's reports cannot be entirely discounted, especially since Etherege in his verse epistles to

Buckhurst and his letters in the 1680s presents many of the same sorts of gross adventures and activities, but under color of high-spirited youth or libertine middle age.

She Would If She Could

Between his first play in 1664 and his second in 1668 there is hardly an event in Etherege's life that can be determined with any certainty, not even where he was living during those years—whether in London or in the country or abroad. Sometime in 1664, to be sure, another of his poems began circulating in manuscript, "To Her Excellence the Marchioness of Newcastle After the Reading of Her Incomparable Poems,"[78] a piece of iambic-pentameter flattery by which he may have hoped to gain favor with the marchioness or her husband. Also in 1664 the first edition of *The Comical Revenge* was printed, having been licensed for the press on 8 July. It was followed by a second edition later the same year and by a third edition in 1667. The first of the many songs to be printed in anthologies during the seventeenth century also appeared in this latter year, "To a Lady, Asking Him How Long He Would Love Her," but when it was written cannot be determined, nor can we learn what other poems may have been composed during the period.

It is possible, of course, that Etherege was in Paris in the summer of 1667—as Gosse speculated—where he may have seen *Tartuffe* performed; and what we know from his letters in the 1680s of his interest in family matters may allow us to imagine him traveling down to Old Windsor to attend his grandfather Powney's funeral in August 1667. But these are the most tentative of speculations.

What is certain is that during those years he was much in the company of Buckhurst, Buckingham, and Sedley, and that his second comedy was written with their encouragement. They were, after all, the friends whom he gathered about him on the afternoon of Ash Wednesday, 6 February 1668, when *She Would If She Could* opened at the Duke's House in Lincoln's Inn Fields before one of the most crowded audiences in that theater's six-and-a-half-year history. Pepys's account of the opening performance is unusually full and is especially valuable because it provides an explanation for the failure of the play:

I to the Duke of York's playhouse; where a new play of Etherige's, called *She Would If She Could;* and though I was there by two o'clock, there was 1000 people put back that could not have room in the pit: and I at last, because my wife was there, made shift to get into the 18*d*. box, and there saw; but, Lord! how full was the house, and how silly the play, there being nothing in the world good in it, and few people pleased in it. The King was there; but I sat mightily behind, and could see but little, and hear not all.

When the play was over, Pepys went looking for his wife but couldn't find her because of the dark and a rainstorm that kept him indoors for an hour and a half. So he wandered about the theater, listening to the conversation of the wits:

And, among the rest, here was the Duke of Buckingham to-day openly sat in the pit;[79] and there I found him with my Lord Buckhurst, and Sidly, and Etherige, the poet; the last of whom I did hear mightily find fault with the actors, that they were out of humour, and had not their parts perfect, and that Harris did do nothing, nor could so much as sing a ketch in it; and so was mightily concerned: while all the rest did, through the whole pit, blame the play as a silly, dull thing, though there was something very roguish and witty; but the design of the play, and end, mighty insipid.

Although Pepys saw the play again a year later, he had nothing more to say about it. Thomas Shadwell, however, writing in the preface to his comedy *The Humorists* (1671), confirms Etherege's complaint: the poor acting, Shadwell said, "had like to have destroyed *She Would If She Could,* which I think (and I have the authority of some of the best judges in England for 't) is the best comedy that has been written since the Restoration of the Stage. . . . Had it not been for the favour of the Court, in all probability it had never got up again; and it suffers for it, in a great measure to this very day."

Shadwell's evaluation of *She Would If She Could* might have been somewhat prejudiced since his wife Ann Gibbs Shadwell had played the role of Lady Cockwood. Among the other actresses was Mary Davis as Gatty, the madcap sister who loves to dance. "Moll" Davis was already one of King Charles's mistresses and would shortly leave the stage, probably right after her performance in *She Would If She Could* at Court on 29 May 1668.[80] On that date Pepys reported that "when she was to come to dance her jigg, the Queene would not stay to see it." The role of Gatty's less lively sister Ariana was taken by Mrs. Jennings,[81] who three years later likewise left the theater, "by force of Love . . . erept the stage," said John Downes (p. 35). Among the men whom Downes names as members of the cast were three who had taken important parts in *The Comical Revenge:* William Smith as Courtall, James Nokes as Sir Oliver Cockwood, and Henry Harris as Sir Joslin Jolley. The last important role, that of Freeman, was taken by John Young, who typically portrayed noble young gentlemen. Pepys didn't like him at all, however, calling him "a bad actor at best," but that judgment—recorded in the *Diary* the previous October—came after Pepys had seen Young act the role of Macbeth in the place of Pepys's favorite, Betterton.

She Would If She Could, however, seems not to have recovered from its inauspicious beginning, despite an excellent company of actors and a premiere that was at least a major social event. Only ten more performances during Etherege's lifetime are recorded in *The London Stage,* and the histories of drama of the time do not suggest that the play was popular. In the first third of the eighteenth century, on the other hand, it was frequently produced, oftentimes as a benefit performance for an actor.[82] Its writing and performance, nevertheless, gave Etherege additional prestige at court and very likely contributed to the next stage in his career.

Between Plays, 1668–1676

One of the court favors that came to Etherege following the production on Ash Wednesday of *She Would If She Could* was his appointment on 31 July as one of the forty-eight Gentlemen of the Privy Chamber in Ordinary to King Charles II.[83] Another was his appointment as secretary to Sir Daniel Harvey, the newly named ambassador to Turkey. It may be, as Eleanor Boswell speculates, that Etherege was given the place at court in order to have suitable standing as the secretary in Sir Daniel's office. Certainly Sir Daniel's was a position of great importance, for at this time it was the only English mission abroad with the rank of embassy and hence it brought with it the highest rank and salary. We do not know the sequence of the appointments, however, whether Etherege was proposed as Gentleman before Secretary, or the other way around. Probably the playwright would need no greater credentials for foreign service than his two comedies, his friendship with the most influential young courtiers of the day, and his many years of legal training, first under George Gosnold and then at Clement's Inn; but he was also the stepson of Christopher Newstead, one-time chaplain to Charles I and to a former ambassador to Constantinople, and those connections may have clinched the matter.

Everything known about Etherege's reactions to life among the Turks is contained in a single remarkable letter that he wrote at the midpoint of his two-year stay in Constantinople. A detailed study by Thomas H. Fujimura provides the background for the adventure and concludes that Etherege's career as secretary to Harvey from the summer of 1668 to the spring of 1671 was a responsible and demanding one, and that it prepared him well for his assignment in 1685 as King James II's envoy to Ratisbon.[84] It certainly contributed also to increasing his knowledge of the world and human society and played some part in shaping the final product of his dramatic genius, *The Man of Mode*.

By 1 May 1671 Etherege was in Paris, after an arduous overland journey, amusing his acquaintances with witty stories about his adventures. William Perwich, English Agent in Paris, wrote on that date that "Etheridge that made *Love in a Tub* [*The Comical Revenge*] is here & contributes extremely to our divertisement."[85] Not long after, it appears, he was back in London, playing the poet-rake once again. In September his quarrel with Ashton took place, and on 9 November his prologue to Dryden's *Sir Martin Mar-all* was read at the grand opening of the new theater in Dorset Garden, which had been built for the Duke's Men. According to tradition the playhouse had been designed by Christopher Wren, and Etherege made its spacious grandeur the principal issue in his prologue. It is no longer possible, he said, for wit alone to draw audiences; now there must be stately theaters and gaudy sights. And the owners of the playhouse (chief among them Etherege's good friend Thomas Betterton) do not care what the audience think of the playwrights. Said the prologue to the audience: "Be kind, and let our House have but your praise, / You're welcome every day to damn their plays."[86] Given his rich sense of irony, Etherege no doubt smiled to himself four-and-a-half years later, recalling these words, when his own play *The Man of Mode* opened in stately Dorset Garden.

Until the acting of the last comedy to come from his pen virtually nothing is known of Etherege's whereabouts and activities. Three days after the performance of *Sir Martin Mar-all* the Duke's Men performed *The Comical Revenge* again, perhaps in return for his providing the Prologue for Dryden. John Downes says *The Comical Revenge* was presented "two days together to a full audience," and it may have gone longer. In the following year, 1672, nine of Etherege's verses were printed with some by his friends Sir Charles Sedley and Lord Buckhurst in Hobart Kemp's *A Collection of Poems,* and he may have had some part in preparing them for the press. Among them were "A Prologue Spoken at the Opening of the Duke's New Playhouse" and Etherege's most popular poem "Silvia" ("Who sees her must love and who loves her must die").[87] In 1673 there are but two notices of Etherege's activities: Dryden mentioned in a letter in May that his friend was translating a satire of Boileau,[88] and according to a manuscript note by William Oldys, in that year Etherege was a witness to Sir William Paul's earlier knighting.[89] As it happens, Paul was from Bray, the parish where Etherege's parents had been married, and he was married to Mary Powney, Etherege's first cousin once removed. As his later letters show, Etherege was much concerned about family affairs, and the favor to Paul is one more evidence of that concern.

Did Etherege go back to Beaconsfield for the burial of his mentor George Gosnold on 1 April 1675? If so, he could have visited family and friends in Maidenhead at the same time, a trip of only nine or ten miles. His mother was almost certainly still living in Maidenhead, for she is recorded in the Bray Parish register as being of that town at the time of her death in 1699. Whatever else he was doing in 1675, however, Etherege was writing a play, for in the following year his masterpiece *The Man of Mode* was produced; it was to make him famous all over again and perhaps for all time.

The Man of Mode

Etherege and the managers of the Duke's Company planned with great care for a success with *The Man of Mode*. There would be no repetition of the failed opening of *She Would If She Could,* with the cast underrehearsed and no prologue or epilogue to charm the audience into the warmest reception possible. When *The Man of Mode* opened at the Dorset Garden Theatre on 11 March,[90] a prologue by Sir Car Scroope invited the audience to observe in the mirror of the stage the same follies that they admired in their mirrors at home; and the best-known of all London playwrights, John Dryden, contributed an epilogue. Betterton himself took the lead role of Dorimant and cast his wife as Bellinda. It may be that the duchess of York helped to pay the cost of extra rehearsals and of the elegant costumes used,[91] for the printed version later on was dedicated to her, and in that dedication Etherege announced that he had written *The Man of Mode* in her service and that it was indebted to her support "for the success it had in the acting." The king's presence, too, at the opening underscored the social importance of the event and helped to assure its solid success.[92]

Among the other well-known actors besides the Bettertons whom Downes lists as having roles in the comedy were Henry Harris playing Medley and William Smith as Sir Fopling Flutter. It was the third Etherege play in which each man had a specially created role. The part of Young Bellair was performed by Thomas Jevon, who had thrown Elkanah Settle into a fit the previous season with his practical joking,[93] and that of Old Bellair was taken by the corpulent Anthony Leigh, who (said Dryden) had legs like timber-logs "that stood strutting like the two black posts before a door."[94] Among the women's roles, says Downes, Mrs. Elinor Leigh played Lady Woodvill, Mrs. Twyford portrayed Emilia, and Elizabeth Barry (the mistress of the earl of Rochester) took the part of the anguished Mrs. Loveit. Although she was a relative newcomer to the stage, being now in her third season, Barry had very likely already developed those qualities of delivery that made her so very appropriate for the part: a voice (said Cibber about her much later) "full, clear, and strong, so that no Violence of Passion could be too much for her."[95]

Many in the audience on that opening night and at subsequent performances were titillated by the sight of the overpassionate Mrs. Loveit being rejected very coldly by her lover Dorimant, who in dress and actions resembled the well-known Lord Rochester. The identification of Rochester with Dorimant was very likely intentional, a part of the design by Etherege and the managers to assure the success of *The Man of Mode*. Betterton dressed himself to resemble Rochester, it is said,[96] and mimicked the earl's mannerisms and speech, repeating the verses of Edmund Waller as Rochester commonly did. Others in the play invited identification as well, and Oldys reported some of them: Sir Fopling Flutter as Sir George Hewitt and Medley as Etherege himself. "Even the shoemaker," says Oldys, "got vast Trade by this Representation of him."[97] More likely, as the similarity of the names suggests, Medley was intended to represent Sir Charles Sedley, but the important thing was that people were talking about the play, even when they disagreed about the identifications. In his epilogue to the play Dryden encouraged such identifications by "protesting too much":

> True fops help nature's work, and go to school
> To file and finish God a'mighty's fool.

> Yet none Sir Fopling him, or him, can call:
> He's knight o' th' shire and represents ye all.

The careful planning of Etherege and the managers, the prologue and epilogue, the thorough rehearsals, and the successful effort to encourage the audience to identify the play's characters with real people, all contributed to the great success that *The Man of Mode* enjoyed at Dorset Garden. Downes says, simply, that it was "well acted [and] got a great deal of money," and Charles Gildon calls its success "extraordinary."[98] The play's stage history is incomplete throughout the rest of the century, but it was regularly performed until the 1750s when it disappeared from the stage, with only one revival, in 1793, before the twentieth century. For Etherege the play's success meant a nice income from a succession of author's nights, and the writing of this play may also have meant a pension of one hundred pounds per year from the duke of York or from the Duchess, Mary of Modena, whom Etherege claimed as his patron.[99] No accomplishment during the rest of his life would be as rewarding or as satisfying as the writing and acting of *The Man of Mode*.

We catch only fleeting glimpses of George Etherege for the next nine years, until late 1685 when he began to turn out the flood of letters from Ratisbon to England that give us such insights into his life and character. There was the disturbance at Epsom in June 1676 and the fight with Bulkeley the following year. A little later in the 1670s, probably in 1679, Etherege was knighted and not long afterward married. According to the *Dictionary of National Biography,* the scandal of the time had it that "he had to buy the honour in order to persuade a rich widow to marry him." The earliest reference to such a title for Etherege is a letter from Charles Hatton to his brother, dated 15 January 1680, reporting that "Sir George Etherege" and several others have been "very dangerously hurt" in the fall of a tennis-court roof.[100] That the knighthood had been conferred very recently is confirmed by Anthony à Wood, who reports the same accident, but refers to "Sir Charles Sidley, George Etheridg, and others," with no mention of a title for Etherege.[101] Recent searches in the official registers of the College of Arms by both Hubert Chesshyre, Chester Herald of Arms, and Conrad Swan, York Herald of Arms, have failed to turn up arms or pedigrees in the name of Etherege. The heralds note, however, that a "reputable" compilation by W. A. Shaw, *Knights of England,* does include the name George Etherege and the date 1680; but the date is followed by a question mark, and no further information is provided. The first published reference to "Sir George," it seems, comes in William Winstanley's *Lives of the Most Famous English Poets* (1687), and thereafter the title is attached to his name with increasing regularity in print.

As to Etherege's rich widow, most of what is known about her comes from three sources: contemporary satiric verses, documents that relate to her first marriage and money dealings, and Etherege's one letter to her and several references in other letters.[102] She was Mary Sheppard Arnold, born about 1628, the widow of successful London attorney Edmund Arnold, who had received his law degree from Oxford in 1661. Two sons had been born to that union, the first in 1648, but both were dead by 1673, and Arnold had died in 1676 and had been buried at his manor in Northamptonshire. The income from this manor he had left to Mary, and with that and the estate she had received from her father she was no doubt justly considered to be rich.

Whether the gossip was true that Etherege married her only for her money, he thought enough of her and kept close enough track of affairs at home to write her more than two dozen letters during the three-and-a-half years he was abroad as English resident in Ratisbon from 1685 to 1689. The single existing letter to Lady Etherege does not, it is true, suggest that the marriage was a love match. In it Sir George apologizes ironically for giving her advice and promises no longer to sign himself as her loving husband but rather as her dutiful husband. This was, however, the only such letter to be copied down by the ambitious and often malicious Hugo Hughes, Etherege's secretary, and so the relationship between husband and wife was probably more congenial than this one piece of correspondence suggests. Etherege's solicitude for his wife's health, expressed in a letter to Owen Wynne, with a request that Wynne deliver a message personally to her, gives a rather different picture. In short, to rely on Hughes and London gossip for accurate information about Etherege is like relying on the *National Enquirer* for information about a contemporary American writer. In both instances, credibility is in short supply.

Ratisbon and Death in Paris

To be able to know in detail about young Etherege's education in Maidenhead in the 1640s or his apprenticeship in Beaconsfield in the 1650s or his way of life in London when he was writing *The Comical*

Revenge—that would be fascinating indeed, if only to enable us to see much more fully the influences upon his literary career. The best-known period in Sir George's life, however, is none of these but is rather that period near the end of his life when he was no longer writing plays and no longer living the life of a court wit in London. The pictures of life in Ratisbon that emerge from his letters home and from four letters by Hughes, his secretary, differ in point of view, to be sure, but probably not in the essential details.[103] Very simply, Etherege, King James's representative to the Holy Roman Empire, tried to live in the staid capital of Ratisbon in the same way he had lived in lively London. In the process he scandalized the diplomatic community and provided ammunition for Hughes to use in an attempt to discredit him in England.

During the first year of his stay in Ratisbon Etherege managed to break most of the rules of conduct that should be expected of the official representative of an important sovereign nation. His love of gambling pursued him from England to Holland and thence to the south of Germany, where he gradually collected about him a gang of gamesters who ate and drank night and day at his expense until one of them—a professional gambler from Vienna who called himself Count Purpurat—won from him eight hundred florins and a pair of specially made pistols that bore Sir George's coat of arms. Moreover, the gamesters carried their quarreling and wrangling out into the city where, said Hughes, they would "walk about the Streets with clubs in their hands to guard themselves and their Musick" (*Letters,* 294). This conduct was only the beginning. Etherege next took up with a French oboe player, and together with other hangers-on, they would spend whole nights at some tavern or would "torment the whole Town with Coaching, fidling, piping, and dancing till 2, 3, and 4 a clock in the morning" (*Letters,* 295). The irate wife of one of the diplomats there, the Countess de Windischgrätz, finally hired a gang to beat them and put a stop to their carousing, but Etherege and company managed to escape.

Etherege's sexual adventures in particular attracted attention, and Hughes recorded them carefully in a duplicate letterbook. Etherege first took up with two sisters, keeping each of them in turn during his first year in Ratisbon. They were followed by an actress from Nuremberg, whom Etherege courted publicly, as if he had been in London, even taking her to the theater. "Sometimes after the play was ended," Hughes wrote in scorn, "he has putt her into his coach before all the

Company notwithstanding all the giggling and hishing of the Austrian Ladys and of the Ministers wives and Daughters, himself humbly walking home on foot" (*Letters,* 300). The affair quickly became a scandal. First the Baron de Sensheim and a gang in disguise tried to take the actress by force from Etherege's house, but he drove them off in a noisy running battle that passed through the heart of town. Thereafter for a time, said Hughes, Etherege traveled about Ratisbon with armed footmen and a musket in his coach, in readiness for the baron; and the actress visited him disguised as a soldier—until she discovered that he had run out of money and left him.

So much for Etherege's first year as a rake in Ratisbon, according to Hughes's account. Unfortunately, Etherege's own letters bear out much of what was charged. He frequently confesses his addiction to gambling and his pursuit of easy women. By late 1687, however, he had at least learned discretion as regards the latter for he wrote to a friend, "The Town is too little to hide us and the liberty of talking is too great, so that poor lovers like Hares in releifing time are fain to clicket up and down in the Gardens at Midnight." And a year later: "I have learn'd . . . to content my self in private with a piece of houshold bread."[104] Hints here and there in the letters, however, suggest that from time to time he suffered from a venereal disease during the Ratisbon period and had so suffered in England previously, and so his amours were not without their unpleasant effects on his health. Hughes, in fact, described Etherege in a doggerel lampoon as "decayed with pox,"[105] but there is no confirmation of so serious a condition.

There were, however, many other entertainments for a gentleman in Ratisbon, and a catalogue of Etherege's amusements there suggests the variety of ways in which the wits in London must also have passed the time. On Sir George's staff were a dancing master and a fencing master, and several skilled in music, and so there must have been a great deal of home entertainment. He often went hunting on horseback, the best diversion the climate afforded, he said, and from time to time would "bungle away a morning" at tennis. Besides the pleasures of conversation at the house of the Comte de Crécy, the French envoy and Etherege's favorite among the diplomats at Ratisbon, there were quiet games of ombre and piquet, and even much time for reading. Etherege's own library numbered near one hundred volumes, most of them in French, and he had access to many more. When the weather was bad and the Diet was not in session, he said, "Reading is the most constant and best entertainement I have . . ." (*Letters,* 189).

As a diplomat he was probably a success, in spite of the gossip and occasional scandal. His principal task was to gather information that could be useful in England's foreign affairs, and he was scrupulous in performing that task, throughout his three-year stay sending to London with each Monday and Thursday post as full an account as possible of current political and military affairs. Much of his correspondence, as a matter of fact, consists of long digests of news that came to him in letters and gazettes from throughout the empire. As mere resident, he held the lowest rank in the diplomatic corps and thus was ineligible to treat officially with the envoys from other nations. Yet, as Frederick Bracher points out, the longer he remained in the position, the more he came to discover that a resident's career could be interesting.[106] His tour de force as the English diplomat in Ratisbon was the magnificient celebration he arranged in honor of the birth of King James's first male heir, the Prince of Wales and Rothesay. Extending over three days, the event displayed more than anything else Etherege did or said his entire loyalty to the Catholic King James. But while the celebration was a diplomatic triumph in Ratisbon, helping Etherege to mend fences with several of the envoys, the birth of the Pretender led shortly after to the Glorious Revolution and James's flight to France. On 19 January 1689, when Sir George received the news of the king's safe arrival in Paris, he wrote to the earl of Carlingford that he intended to join the king very soon. By 20 February he was in Paris.

Probably he had no choice. To return to England was impossible. The trip, even if he could have afforded it, would have been long, arduous, and possibly dangerous, for the times were terribly unsettled and he was well known as an ardent supporter of the deposed king. That he was well aware of the danger is evident in his last letter from Ratisbon. There he commented angrily to Carlingford about the "cruelties and outrages which are acted against the Roman Catholiques" in England. Etherege still had a home in London,[107] could he get there safely, but there were outstanding gambling debts awaiting his return (so his letters suggest) and it would not be a simple matter to reenter the old life of careless leisure. To remain at his post in Ratisbon must also have appeared to him to be out of the question. His deep personal loyalty to King James and to the principle of legal succession would not permit such a course. Moreover, he had the example of his loyal father, who had left him when he was only six or seven in order to follow the queen into France, and who had died there when young George was only fourteen. Hence Etherege's last words from Ratisbon: "[I] intend very suddainly to be with his Majesty, being resolv'd to live and dy in serving him faithfully" (*Letters,* 266).

When Sir George Etherege died in Paris is not certainly known, and the manner of his death is a complete mystery. His last catalogued letters are dated 28 September 1689. They are to his sister, his wife, and a moneylender, and they suggest financial difficulties. Thereafter there is no information. In his edition of *Letters* Frederick Bracher has gathered together most of the few scattered pieces of information relating to Etherege's death. An entry at the Benedictine monastery in Ratisbon indicates that in 1691 he died a Catholic in Paris. The Benedictine abbot, Placid Fleming, was a good friend and should have known if such a conversion had occurred. It is possible, as Bracher speculates, that Etherege spent his last days at the Benedictine College in Paris, run by Abbot Fleming's friend Lewis Innes. Certainly Etherege would have carried a letter of introduction from Fleming to Innes, and he may well have stayed at the college, since his name does not show up on any of the manuscript lists of the exiled English court in Paris.[108]

In February 1691 Lady Etherege's attorney heard a rumor that Etherege was dead, and historian Narcissus Luttrell repeats that report. Other information, equally dubious, comes from playwright Thomas Southerne, who speaks of Etherege as still alive in 1693, and from critic-playwright John Dennis, who in 1721 or 1722 wrote that Etherege has been dead "nearly thirty years" (i.e., he had died in 1692 or 1693).[109] The most trustworthy account of Sir George's death comes from nephew George Etherege, the son of Etherege's younger brother Richard. In 1697, when continuing a lawsuit begun by Sir George, nephew Etherege testified that "on or about the Tenth day of May in the year of our Lord one thousand six hundred and ninety two the said Sr. George Etherege dyed without Issue. . . ."[110] This seems to be the best choice of a date. The two men, uncle and nephew, had been in regular communication by mail during Etherege's term as Resident, and the younger man would almost certainly have known the date of Sir George Etherege's death.

Chapter Two

The Comical Revenge; or, Love in a Tub (1664)

"A New Tone and Attitude"

What was there in George Etherege's first play to make it the most popular comedy to be performed since the restoration of the London stage in 1660? Was it the novelty of his portraying lifelike people in contemporary London settings, as has been frequently suggested, that led to an unprecedented month-long run in March 1664? Or was it that Etherege had cleverly brought together in one comedy the best ingredients of a variety of different well-liked types of drama?

The combination in *The Comical Revenge* of social comedy with serious heroic play and lively farce was doubtless one of the reasons for its success. Most of the varied material in the play would have been familiar to audiences in 1664. The admirable heroic lovers, for example, a type that seems to modern readers too idealistic for comedy, had been seen recently in Sir William Davenant's popular plays; and viewers would have been sympathetic to their blank-verse sentiments, believing with Davenant that providing "characters of Vertue in the shapes of Valour and Conjugal Love" was a primary purpose of the drama.[1]

The wit-combat scenes of the gay couple, too, would have been familiar from the *English Mounsieur* of the previous season,[2] as well as from the older plays—from Francis Beaumont and John Fletcher and certainly from such characters as Shakespeare's Beatrice and Benedict in *Much Ado About Nothing* and Petruchio and Katherina in *The Taming of the Shrew*. The plays of Beaumont and Fletcher would have been especially familiar, as Louis B. Wright has noted, because their dramatic works were the most widely read during the Commonwealth.[3] Confidence schemes of all sorts, too, were familiar from the older dramatic literature, some of the most notable examples to be found in Ben Jonson's *The Alchemist* and *Volpone*. Even the use of rhymed couplets in the upper plot of the play was not new, having been used in

Davenant's *The Siege of Rhodes* and in the recently produced *The Indian Queen* (25 January 1664), Sir Robert Howard's and John Dryden's heroic drama. And scenes of farce, masquing, dance, and music would have been found wholesale in the plays familiar to the audiences of the time.

So far Etherege can at least lay claim to a remarkable eclecticism. But what in *The Comical Revenge* can really be called new? Only a handful of other new comedies had appeared since the opening of the theaters, and scholars have agreed that none of them were novel enough or successful enough with audiences to have contributed to the development of the drama of the next era. In his study of the comedies from the pre-Restoration period as they influenced the next period, Gunnar Sorelius concludes that two of the new plays—Dryden's *The Wild Gallant* (1663) and Etherege's first comedy, *The Comical Revenge*—"were about the only indications that English comedy was entering upon a new era."[4] The influence of *The Wild Gallant,* of course, was slight because it was a failure, whereas Etherege's comedy was an outstanding success. Robert D. Hume, agreeing that the gay couple and the rhymed heroic drama were familiar from the old plays, points to *The Comical Revenge*—with *The Indian Queen* and *The English Mounsieur*—as representing a "new tone and attitude" in Restoration drama.[5] Although it seems to have been only moderately popular, James Howard's *The English Mounsieur* is the more important of the latter two plays, in part because of its possible influence on Etherege. Its plot is based upon the rocky courting of Widow Wealthy by a wild young man-about-town named Welbred. In the love duel between the two, says John Harrington Smith, "the gay-couple pattern appears full-blown" and is in essence something new in Restoration drama. Hence *The Comical Revenge,* he concludes, is less important than had been averred because the central action of that play is anticipated in Howard's play.[6]

At the same time, however, we must acknowledge the one new ingredient in Etherege's popular play. That ingredient is, of course, the character of Sir Frederick Frollick, Etherege's hard-drinking, window-smashing, whore-chasing, practical-joking, manipulative hero. As a representative of the type that Robert Jordan calls "the extravagant rake,"[7] Sir Frederick might have stepped out of the streets of London and onto the stage, might indeed have been inspired in large degree by real-life rakes as well as literary ones, Lord Buckhurst and friends, for example, whose exploits at the Cock Tavern and elsewhere were common gossip at the time Etherege was writing *The Comical Revenge*. Sir Frederick, however, unlike previous dramatic rakes, including Howard's Welbred, stands out as the hero in control of two social worlds, the low-life world of the London streets and the heroic world of Sir Bevill and his honor-ridden family. When the coarse realism of the poxed Dufoy and his sweating tub was added to the mix, Etherege's audience must have been convinced that something new in theatrical fare was being offered to them.

That Sir Frederick Frollick is more than simply the noisy hero of one part in a four-part play can be seen by examining the amount of time he spends on stage, the number of lines he is given, and the degree to which he is involved in the other parts. In all three ways he is dominant. He is on stage longer and has more lines than any other character, and he is the principal agent in all four plots, bringing the three lower plots to a close, and helping to close the fourth by serving as master of the revels that celebrate the engagements of the two couples in the heroic story—and his own engagement.

Plot Summary

An overview of the action of *The Comical Revenge* will indicate how thoroughly Sir Frederick Frollick is in control of events, and it will serve as a starting point for further discussion.

Act 1. The comic main plot introduces the action of the play. Because of Sir Frederick's drunken escapade the night before, his house is besieged this morning by fiddlers, coachmen, and linkboys (torch bearers) to whom he owes money. Sending his French servant Dufoy to pay their bills, Frollick listens to the complaint of Jenny, Mrs. Grace's maid, that he had tried noisily to enter their house the night before and that now their reputation is damaged and they must find a new apartment. The wittiest line in the play is Sir Frederick's response to their impending move: "And thou art come to tell me whither;—kind heart!" It is lucky for him, she continues, that Grace's lover Wheadle was not there. Nevertheless, she invites him to their lodging later on.

Sir Frederick's cousin Beaufort arrives in time to hear of these adventures. When he asks about Wheadle, Sir Frederick reports that he is a gambler and confidence man who is presently at work gulling one Sir Nicholas Cully, an ambitious oaf who was knighted by Cromwell. Beaufort's love affairs are now over, he says, for he is engaged to marry the divine Graciana, daughter of the Lord Bevill. Although Frollick laughs at the young man's lovesick enthusiasm, he accepts an invitation to dine with him at Lord Bevill's. But Sir Frederick is apprehensive when he learns that the Widow Rich, sister to Lord Bevill, hopes to see him there. While he does not love her, he is attracted by her wealth.

The next scene introduces the first of the comic subplots, Wheadle's and Palmer's gulling of Sir Nicholas Cully. By promising that they will find a willing woman for him, Wheadle arranges to meet Cully later that afternoon at the Devil tavern.

The last scene in act 1 opens the heroic upper plot at Lord Bevill's house. In spite of her declared love for Beaufort, Graciana is urged by her sister Aurelia—and later by her brother Lovis—to accept as her suitor the noble Bruce, imprisoned by Oliver Cromwell as a murderer. Lovis supports Bruce because he is his best friend, Aurelia because she loves him herself.

Act 2. After a second comic subplot is introduced, a brief scene in which Dufoy reveals to Beaufort's servant Clark that he has the pox, and then counterfeits a passion for the widow's maid Betty in order to explain his pale complexion, the comic main plot continues with an exchange between Sir Frederick and the widow in which she hints at marriage and he pretends lack of interest.

Meanwhile, Graciana reveals to Beaufort that she has been courted by her brother's friend Bruce and that her father has promised her to him, but only if she returns Bruce's love. When Graciana and Beaufort leave, with Sir Frederick and the Widow Rich, Aurelia confesses to her maid her love for the imprisoned cavalier. Next the Cully subplot proceeds apace, as Palmer pretends to be a rich farmer and he and Wheadle lead their dupe into a game of dice.

Act 3. Cully has now lost one thousand pounds to Palmer but refuses to pay, arguing that he thought it was only a friendly game. As part of their plan to frighten him into paying, Palmer challenges him to a duel the next morning.

Having spent the evening at the park with the widow, Sir Frederick now goes to her home to serenade her. To prevent his waking the neighbors with fiddles and singing, she invites him in, and his linkboys turn out to be dancers who perform a masque for her. After some badinage about her widowed state and some brisk returns on her part, he marches his company off.

Wheadle and the terrified Cully prepare to fight the duel with

Palmer, but at the last moment the cowardly Cully agrees to pay the debt. Wheadle serves as cosigner.

The three scenes that follow contrast sharply with the comic subplots, for they move rapidly toward a bloody confrontation between Beaufort and Bruce. Lovis has been unsuccessful in his attempts to persuade his father to order Graciana to marry Bruce, and when Bruce is suddenly released from prison, Lovis and Aurelia reluctantly inform him that the woman he loves is engaged to Beaufort. At Lovis's urging, Bruce confronts the two lovers in Lord Bevill's garden and challenges Beaufort to a duel. When Bruce is gone, Graciana pleads with Beaufort not to fight.

Act 4. After a brief scene in which Lovis formally delivers Bruce's challenge and Sir Frederick agrees to be Beaufort's second, the Cully subplot continues with a new scheme by Palmer and Wheadle to extract even more money from Sir Nicholas. Palmer will disguise himself as Lord Bevill, and Grace (Wheadle's mistress) will pretend to be the Widow Rich. The plan is to convince Cully to disguise himself as Sir Frederick in the expectation of marrying the widow so that he can pay his gambling debt to Palmer. When the marriage is consummated, the gang intends to fleece Cully of his estate.

At the scene of the Beaufort-Bruce duel four assassins and their colonel are awaiting the opportunity to avenge Bruce's killing of the colonel's father at the battle of Naseby in 1645. It was the colonel, too, who was responsible for Bruce's imprisonment by suborning perjury. When the men attack Bruce and Lovis, however, Beaufort and Sir Frederick drive the villains away, and so it is now Beaufort who must urge the duel onward, for Bruce is unwilling to draw his sword against the man who has just saved his life. They fight, however, and Bruce is disarmed. In despair at having lost Graciana forever, he abruptly falls upon his sword, inflicting a dangerous wound. Sir Frederick prevents Beaufort from following suit.

Lord Bevill brings to Graciana the rumor that Bruce has killed himself for her, and when Beaufort arrives, she announces to him that her love has turned to hate because he fought Bruce despite her pleading.

Two scenes of comic counterpoint now follow. In the first the widow's waiting-woman Betty punishes Dufoy for his false profession of love and for having the pox by drugging him and imprisoning him with his head thrust out of a wooden tub. In the second Sir Frederick has himself delivered as if dead to the widow's, but his effort thus to make her confess her love for him is interrupted by Dufoy's arrival in the tub, and her laughter at Frollick's discomfiture turns the tables and leaves him embarrassed.

Act 5. Aurelia admits her hopeless love to the wounded Bruce, and he responds gallantly that he would have courted her had he known of her passion. As a consequence, when Graciana enters, confessing that she has sinned against his noble love for her, Bruce attempts to convince her that Beaufort and she belong to each other. But Graciana does not yet see that Bruce already loves Aurelia, and so she scorns Beaufort when he throws himself before her.

There is another meeting of comic plots when the drunken Cully comes to visit the supposed widow and ends up at the house of the real widow. Before the Widow Rich can drive Cully away, however, Sir Frederick puts into execution another of his schemes to embarrass her and test her love. He pretends to have been arrested for debt. The Widow Rich pays the two hundred pounds he owes and has him brought to her house, but Dufoy reveals the cheat when, released from his tub at the widow's request, he attacks the bailiffs and shows them to be Sir Frederick's fiddlers. This time it is the widow who is angry, and Sir Frederick insults her further by promising to spend the two hundred pounds on wine and women. When she leaves, he reveals to the drunken Sir Nicholas Cully both plots to cheat the knight, and he gets Palmer to confess. Sir Frederick promises, tongue-in-cheek, to marry his own wealthy sister to Cully.

The last three scenes of the comedy bring the four plots to their resolutions. In the upper plot Beaufort overhears Graciana confess that she loves him and will marry him if Bruce lives. Beaufort is pleased because he is certain that Bruce will recover. Next Sir Frederick confronts Wheadle with the one-thousand-pound debt that he and Cully had cosigned to pay to Palmer and that Palmer has now signed over to Sir Frederick. To avoid prosecution, Wheadle agrees to marry his mistress Grace; Palmer will wed her maid Jenny.

In the final scene Lord Bevill gives Aurelia to Bruce and Graciana to Beaufort, and he brings Sir Frederick and his sister, Widow Rich, to an agreement to marry—after the two have done a little more verbal fencing. In his turn, Sir Frederick calls in the three couples he has linked together, making the point to the widow that he has now given his own cast-off mistress Lucy to Sir Nicholas Cully—to the latter's dismay. Sir Frederick's gift of money to Dufoy brings that episode to its only plausible end, and Lord Bevill ends all by turning his house over to Sir Frederick to direct the celebration of the three sets of engagements and the three sets of marriages.

Sir Frederick Frollick

While a synopsis can give an overview of the essential action in *The Comical Revenge,* it cannot indicate accurately how completely Sir Frederick's presence fills the stage. He participates in nearly forty percent of the scenes; he manages most of the situations as well as the conclusion of the play; and he is responsible for a remarkable set of masques, songs, and dances that dominate many of the scenes. Jocelyn Powell, citing Samuel Pepys's comment that the comedy was "very merry, but only so by gesture, not wit at all,"[8] concludes that Sir Frederick, in this latter aspect of his role, served as a unifying presence. The scenes to which Pepys referred by the term "gesture" would have been created, says Powell, principally by the actions of Sir Frederick Frollick, and would have resulted in "a unity of mood . . . by extravagance and stylisation of gesture, making a dramatic fantasy of sheer exhilaration and enjoyment."[9] Even in the heroic plot, taking about a third of the play, the acting was done in stately and stylized movements, and that would have contributed further to the unity of "gesture."

Although the escapades of Sir Frederick, the "frolics" that give him his name in the play, may not perfectly tie together the heroic world and the realistic world, they do fill the stage at frequent intervals with lively dance and music and serve to bring the comedy to an end in the same joyous manner. The earliest promise of such entertainment to come is found in Dufoy's announcement of the "regiment" of coachmen, linkboys, and fiddlers waiting for their pay outside Sir Frederick's lodgings and threatening momentarily to enter upon the stage. The frolics begin in earnest in 3.2 with the arrival on stage of Sir Frederick and his fiddlers, "and six or eight LINKBOYS, dancing and singing." In this scene the fiddlers sing a song and in the following scene join the linkboys to perform a masque for the widow.

Sir Frederick's next entertainment, in 4.7, is interrupted before the fiddlers, disguised as pall bearers, can begin. Dufoy, struggling with his tub, so startles them that they run out, followed shortly by their embarrassed master. In 5.2 the mock-Sir Frederick (Sir Nicholas Cully) enters with his own musical entertainment and a crowd of hooting boys; this scene is followed by still another attempt by Sir

Frederick and his fiddlers, now disguised as bailiffs, to perform for the widow. They are interrupted by Dufoy, helmet on head and sword in hand, but this time they end up playing while Dufoy dances a jig. The scene closes with marching and countermarching by the fiddlers, who first follow Sir Frederick out, tag after him when he returns with Palmer in tow, and then follow their master out once again with Palmer as their prisoner. Two scenes later the fiddlers, still in disguise, march in to arrest Wheadle, and march out with him and Cully. They make their final appearance at Lord Bevill's when Sir Frederick calls them in to perform, still disguised as bailiffs and probably accompanied by the dancing masters, still disguised as linkboys.

All of this lively action, besides pleasing with its mixture of boisterous and graceful energy, serves to reinforce Sir Frederick in his role as the dominant presence in the comedy. Moreover, and more important, while he brings with him into many scenes these displays of energy, he also serves to moderate some of the excesses in the upper and lower plots. Early in act 1, when he tells Beaufort about Wheadle, the confidence man, Sir Frederick speaks scornfully of Wheadle as one whose ambition has led him to all sorts of extravagant conduct. Coming from one who has just been introduced as a man who himself is guilty of extravagant conduct among the constables and glass windows of London, this seems ironic. But Sir Frederick's faults of animal high spirits are different in kind from the plotting of the cony-catching Wheadle, and Sir Frederick's intervention after the Cromwellian knight has been sufficiently embarrassed saves Sir Nicholas from the loss of his entire estate. In the same way, Sir Frederick moderates the extremes of the upper plot, beginning with his prosaic response to the heroic Beaufort's iambic-pentameter report of his impending marriage:

BEAUFORT. I have been hitherto so prosperous,
My happiness has still outflown my faith:
Nothing remains but ceremonial charms,
Graciana's fixed i'th' circle of my arms.

SIR FREDERICK. Then y'are a happy man for a season.

BEAUFORT. For ever.

SIR FREDERICK. I mistrust your mistress's divinity; you'll find her attributes but mortal; women, like jugglers' tricks, appear Miracles to the ignorant; but in themselves th'are mere cheats. (1.1)

Sir Frederick's scorn of Beaufort's bloodless devotion reaches a climax in the duelling scene: he is friend enough to offer his sword as Beaufort's second, despite the folly of the cause and his own lack of practice. Most important, however, he rescues the noble Lovis from worse folly when he, like Bruce, attempts to fall on his sword. "Forbear, sir; the frolic's not to go round, as I take it," says Sir Frederick, coolly.

Despite his name and his reputation for antisocial conduct, Sir Frederick Frollick is clearly a force for social good. His linking of Palmer, Wheadle, and Cully to two whores and a servant girl is a necessary part of the comic equilibrium that needs to be attained by the end of the play, but it is also a solution to the social problem of unattached men and women in society, the men in need of the settling influence of a wife and the women needing economic security. The linking of Palmer and Jenny is especially ingenious because Sir Frederick envisions her as the breadwinner in the family, using her knowledge of exotic wines as a way to make money.

Sir Frederick Frollick's own marriage is the solution to another problem of seventeenth-century society, what to do with the widows of the world—vulnerable as they are to exploitation, hard to marry off even when wealthy, and possessing appetites that may lead them to folly and worse. Moreover, like the men of the comic subplots—and those too of the upper plot—Sir Frederick will be stabilized by marriage; he will settle down, give up drunkenness, break no more windows, and confine himself henceforth to one woman. It may be an unrealistic dream for society, but society dreams it nevertheless.

The Gay Couple

The principal action of *The Comical Revenge* is what John Harrington Smith calls "a sprightly courtship game,"[10] with a gay couple who begin their relationship as antagonists and who retain their prickly defensive outer shells to the very verge of matrimony itself. There is much sex antagonism in the play, but it is wittily exaggerated by a pair of lovers who also like each other and want to learn whether they can make a successful marriage. The wit combats between Sir Frederick and the widow, the subterfuges that he employs in order to test her love, and the patience with which she accepts the odd testaments of his—these are all very funny, just as most courtship is funny, as long as it is somebody else's. It is the kind of love chase that characterizes all of Restoration manners comedy. What an audience finds especially comic about Sir Frederick's courting is that the underdog—the widow—wins in what appears on the surface to be an unequal contest. Sir Frederick, with his charm and good looks, ought to be able to gain the favors of the woman who loves him, without having to resort to marriage. But he cannot, and that is funny. Moreover, despite his professed distrust of women as "mere cheats," he pursues the widow with an enthusiasm that seems intended as much to test her patience and wit as a possible mate as to test her readiness to become a mistress. This disparity between what he professes and what he practices is also very funny, the more so because the woman whom he pursues is an experienced widow rather than a fresh ingenue.

At the same time, the Widow Rich is a member of the aristocracy, sister to Lord Bevill, and thus is not to be treated like a common streetwalker; hence we laugh at Sir Frederick's pretended crudeness, when he speaks a little too frankly of her "kind thoughts of his body" and when he warns Beaufort that her ruin lies on her own head. The scene that follows between Sir Frederick and the widow is a continuation in the same comic vein. He maintains the pretense of being a "vain, idle fellow" unable to converse with "ceremonious ladies." But it is a bantering pretense and not a cruel one. How far can he go before he embarrasses her? He finds out when he suggests that widows are especially passionate and thus most dangerous to bachelors like him, for then the widow calls him rude, but softens her remark by inviting him to walk with her in the garden and afterward in the park.

The mutual testing continues late that night at the widow's house, when Sir Frederick returns with his dancing masters to create a noisy scene outside her window, a paler version of the clamor he had created at Grace's house the night before. On one level, the frolic is a comic inversion of the conventional romantic courtship that required the "whining lover" to stand beneath his mistress's window in rapt adoration or in song.[11] Sir Frederick eschews rapt adoration of his lady, however, and instead tries verses, delivered in a canting tone, that defend the "insolence in love" and offer the mandatory praise of her ocular powers: "Alas, what pains I take thus to unclose / Those pretty eyelids which locked up my foes!" The ironic tone and the farcical setting, with fiddlers and linkboys dancing and singing and Betty hanging out the window, are certain to have a comic effect on the audience, even though Sir Frederick's lines are disturbingly like the serious love speeches in the upper plot, including Beaufort's earlier plaint to Graciana in 2.2:

> Waste not those precious tears; oh, weep no more!
> Should heaven frown the world would be too poor,
> (Robbed of the sacred treasure of your eyes). . . .

The greater interest in the frolic scene lies in the mutual knowledge gained by the gay couple. Sir Frederick already knows that the widow loves him for the "freeness of [his] humour" and his "careless carriage" (1.2); Beaufort had told him that. To prove to her that she's not wrong, he has his fiddlers and dancing masters present a masque that they must have been working on all evening. She approves and his reputation as a wit is reinforced; moreover, she manages the evening judiciously; she orders him away when he first arrives, invites him in when he threatens to disturb the neighborhood, gives warm approval to his frolic, and repulses his overtures with wit and good nature. If this is Sir Frederick's attempt at a seduction, he shows little persistence and less judgment, and that is also funny.

In the interval before his next testing of the widow Sir Frederick's character is given a new dimension of seriousness that increases the audience's respect for him and makes it more likely that his pursuit of her is "honorable" rather than otherwise. When he hears of Beaufort's impending duel, he goes immediately to him, ostensibly to offer his sword, but principally to talk him out of his folly: "But dares so zealous a lover as your lordship break the commandment of your mistress? I heard, poor lady, she wept, and charged you to sleep in a whole skin; but young men never know when th'are well" (4.1). When Beaufort pleads that duty to family requires that he accept the challenge, Sir Frederick's reply is sardonic: "Pray whose body must I exercise my skill upon?" His hindering the distraught Lovis from suicide is, as noted earlier, a further evidence of his good sense. At this point in the play it is clear that Sir Frederick's judgment is superior to that of most of the other characters, and we may speculate that he is older than the young men of the heroic plot. His title indicates that he is a knight or baronet, and he could only have been awarded one of those titles in Charles's time, no later than 1642. Since *The Comical Revenge* takes place during the Protectorate (i.e., after 12 December 1653), Sir Frederick was very likely intended by Etherege to be thought of as in his thirties.

When the courtship game continues again, as it must if the gay couple are to gain the knowledge of each other that they need in order to enter upon marriage, Sir Frederick's next frolic almost succeeds in its design to discover how deeply the Widow Rich loves him, and the sequence of events is deliciously funny. No sooner has Dufoy waddled offstage in his tub than Sir Frederick is borne in, the widow weeping real tears over his supposed corpse. The audience is startled; did the duel resume between Lovis and Sir Frederick, or has there been another ambush, and is this the result? But the Mourner who reports has the details of the duel all wrong and we begin to suspect. Dufoy's sudden irruption and the helter-skelter tumble on stage that follows bring the biggest laughs of the play. The widow's own laughter at Sir Frederick's failed frolic is her comical revenge on him for testing her love in this painful way, for he must now hide his serious interest in her by exaggerating his distress: he will forswear her company, he says, kill her cat, and make her weep for ever after. If she will promise not to smile, however, they can still be friends. Of course she smiles—laughs out loud—and Sir Frederick storms out, hurling a mock curse at her. The widow has won this round, but more important, the two have new knowledge of each other, and what they have learned bodes well for a future together.

The final testing scene will right the imbalance that the widow's victory has created in their relationship. Like the previous scene, with Dufoy in his tub, this one begins with farce—the drunken Cully pursued by a mob of street-boys and Dufoy, still in his tub, threatening to attack the bailiffs who have arrested Sir Frederick. The widow's actions are once again the right ones, Sir Frederick discovers: she pays his debt without hesitating and still desires his company despite his obvious carelessness about business affairs. And when his two-hundred-pound trick is discovered, her pique is as wittily exaggerated as his had been earlier: she will marry Cully in revenge; she will never speak to him again and forbids him ever to visit her. Sir Frederick's reactions confirm for us that he now takes her seriously, for he confesses that he is jealous of Cully's attentions to her (5.2), and he tells Dufoy he will not leave her angry for longer than two hours. After all, fair play permits him his moment of pleasure at outwitting her in turn.

Between this final scene of testing and the denouement, when Lord Bevill joins the hands of Sir Frederick Frollick and the Widow Rich, occurs that series of events in which Sir Frederick seizes control over the rest of the comic world of the play and in the process further demonstrates his good judgment and the likelihood that he will marry the widow. He does not, however, merely prevent Wheadle and Palmer from carrying out their confidence game; he goes well beyond and repairs other rents in the fabric of society. Wheadle must marry; it is the way to tame his extravagance. And he must marry Grace, his whoremistress, so that she too is brought within the bounds of respectability. Wheadle's companion in crime, Palmer, is to be weaned from his criminal ways by means of marriage to Jenny, the servant to Grace. Her marriage portion will be her knowledge of the making of special wines, says Sir Frederick: with it "she shall maintain you, Sir" (5.4). The names of Stiponie and Democcuana—the former a raisin wine, the latter still unknown—remind us that Etherege had lived for most of his youth in the home of his grandfather, a wine merchant before his retirement; there the young man might well have become familiar with such exotic recipes.

The final healing act by Sir Frederick, before his betrothal to the widow, is the marriage he arranges between Sir Nicholas Cully and his own mistress Lucy. Sir Nicholas's dismay in the final scene at the sudden reversal in his fortunes is comic, to be sure, for he thought he had married Sir Frederick's sister. But there are advantages for both of them. Lucy will be taken care of by a man of means, and so she will now be neither a burden on Sir Frederick's conscience nor a threat to his marriage. Even Sir Nicholas may benefit, if he can avoid gossip back home, for Lucy is an accomplished mistress; and should there be gossip, her former connection to one of London's wittiest and most admired men-about-town does not make her entirely despicable.

"Hyperbolical Joy and Outragious Sorrow"

Contrasting sharply in tone with the lively comedy of the three subplots is the upper plot of *The Comical Revenge*. That Etherege intended it to be taken seriously may be difficult for some modern audiences to accept, for its excesses of language and situation are evident in every scene. The great literary critic of the next age, Dr. Samuel Johnson, scorned such drama for its unreality:

> To bring a lover, a lady and a rival into the fable; to entangle them in contradictory obligations, perplex them with oppositions of interest, and harass them with violence of desires inconsistent with each other; to make them meet in rapture and part in agony; to fill their mouths with hyperbolical joy and outragious sorrow, to distress them as nothing human ever was distressed; to deliver them as nothing human ever was delivered, is the business of a modern dramatist.[12]

Johnson could have been summarizing the upper plot of *The Comical Revenge*.

Nevertheless, both because the upper plot acted out beliefs important to the Cavaliers and to Etherege personally, as has been indicated previously, and because it was a fashionable style, the audience would have taken the presentation of the heroic Bevill family at face value. Like the modern audience at a Verdi grand opera, the spectators would have willingly suspended their disbelief for the sake of sharing in the rich range of ideals and emotions on display.

It has often been noted by students that in the early years of the Restoration drama was much influenced by the platonic court drama of the previous age. Kathleen Lynch's pioneering study of the Restoration milieu[13] traces both the artificiality of the heroic scenes and the love intrigue of the comic ones to the platonic formalities of the court of Charles I and to his French wife Henrietta Maria. It was she who had introduced the vogue of *préciosité,* a ceremonious system of conversing and making love that is based on the belief that ladies of virtue and beauty have semidivine powers and can raise to a higher spiritual level lovers and even lesser ladies. As Lynch points out, a number of Sir William Davenant's plays were designed to interpret this précieuse cult, and Sir John Suckling's poetry expressed its wit. With the coming of the Civil War all these ceremonial pastimes were brought to an end at court, but they continued in Cavalier society in exile in France and at the Restoration reappeared in the dialogue and attitudes of the new comedy, particularly that of John Dryden and George Etherege.

The presentation on stage of scenes in which the old aristocratic values were portrayed was, of course, much more than mere nostalgia. The upper plot of Etherege's *The Comical Revenge* reflects, as do heroic scenes in other contemporary plays, the emotional need of the Royalists for a justification of their mannered way of life as well as for an imaginary world in which they could somehow win the battles they had lost to the armies of Cromwell. In his study of Restoration critical theory Sarup Singh argues that heroic drama was for the aristocracy a dreamland "where they could find love, virtue, and greatness as a substitute for the pettiness around them." As one evidence, he cites the commendatory verses prefixed to Sir Samuel Tuke's *The Adventures of Five Hours* (1664):

> Finding this Age does want that noble pride,
> For which brave men of old were deify'd:

> In meer compassion to this wretched age
> You bring heroique Vertue on the Stage.[14]

The Comical Revenge also intends to supply a picture of that dreamland of "heroique virtue."

Perhaps the most interesting aspect of that picture is the degree to which Etherege's noble characters speak of the power that fate or heaven has over human affairs. When Aurelia charges that all Graciana needs to do is to *will* her love for Bruce, Graciana retorts that "We of ourselves can neither love nor hate; / Heav'n does reserve the pow'r to guide our fate." Lord Bevill agrees and orders Lovis to be silent on the subject (1.3). When Bruce unexpectedly arrives, he and Aurelia commiserate with each other: Graciana has been misled by unlucky stars, he says; Fate has done its worst, he says. In her brief soliloquy at the end of the scene, however, Aurelia finds that the Fates have had their revenge by making her love Bruce (3.6). When, in the final scene, the two discover that they do love each other, Lord Bevill gives his approval since, he says, the Heavens have already decreed that Bruce and Aurelia should wed. Even Sir Frederick Frollick, the voice of reason in the play, announces in the couplet that closes the comedy that all of them are the creatures of Fate, that "chance, not prudence, makes us fortunate."

Although assigning to Fate the blame for all the accidents on which our lives depend, love included, is an ancient convention in poetry, for the disillusioned courtiers of the 1660s it was a psychological necessity. To credit blind Fate for the failures of the past two decades was far preferable to allowing military superiority to the Puritans or—worse—admitting that God had indeed been on the enemy's side, as the Roundheads had claimed.

Most critics have argued that the upper plot of the heroic Bevill family and the lively lower plot of the gay couple are an unnatural mixture that cannot reasonably be linked together, but that seems not to have been a concern of the audience who first saw *The Comical Revenge*. John Dryden, who may have been in that audience, had a kind word to say about the juxtaposing of the two diverse forms, calling it in the *Essay of Dramatic Poesy* the most pleasant way of writing comedy that was ever known. The sensible word to say is that the high and low plots are joined in the person of Sir Frederick Frollick. Like Prince Hal in *Henry IV, Part I,* he enjoys the low life of London, knowing that he must rejoin the aristocratic life eventually. Sir Frederick is the efficient healer of society's ailments, a role that by twentieth-century standards qualifies him as a real hero; and he moves with ease through the aristocratic society of the noble Bruce and the equally noble Bevill family, knowing that when the young people get over their précieuse folly they will make acceptable members of that society, worthy perhaps of his company and conversation. Lord Bevill, the sage counselor of the heroic plot, admires Sir Frederick, accepts him heartily, and rewards him in the final scene; and Lord Bevill is no fool. Like Grandfather Etherege, he is the stable center of his family, correcting his headstrong son, supporting his daughters in their choices of mates, and at last performing the act of mercy that the audience has been awaiting for five acts: he joins the hands of the old bachelor and the rich widow and thus commits the most significant social act of the play. If the elder Etherege had been as successful with his family, the life of his grandson would have been much altered.

Chapter Three
She Would If She Could (1668)
"A Comedy of Manners Had Arrived"

In his second play George Etherege turned into realistic prose the two pairs of lovers in his first play, lowered their social standing a couple of notches, and put them in the center of the action instead of on the periphery. The result was a much more unified piece than *The Comical Revenge,* but one that turned out to be a theatrical failure by comparison, even though admired by contemporary men of wit. Twentieth-century critics have likewise praised *She Would If She Could* as the first fully developed Restoration comedy of manners, despite the likelihood that it had little influence on contemporary plays: "A comedy of manners had arrived," say Emmett L. Avery and Arthur H. Scouten in *The London Stage,*[1] summing up the pronouncements of many students of Restoration drama from Edmund Gosse on. Dale Underwood calls it "a kind of primer for the later and major comedies of the period."[2] The examination by Professor Hume of the other comedies of the time, however, has revealed no parallels to *She Would If She Could* as a whole, although most of the parts are common stock in trade—in particular the wenching and gaming and the witty gay couples.[3]

It is the uniqueness of *She Would If She Could,* its originality as a series of witty explorations of character within a recognizable London setting, that seems to have impressed Etherege's contemporaries, as it continues to impress twentieth-century critics. Lord Rochester, writing in 1675–1676, said of his friend Etherege that he had never copied great playwrights like Shakespeare and Jonson, "But is himself a sheer original."[4] John Dennis, the early eighteenth-century critic and playwright, argued that Etherege's originality in *She Would If She Could* lay in "the trueness of some of [the] characters, and the purity and freeness and easie grace of [the] dialogue."[5]

If some of the characters of *She Would If She Could* are true to the real world of the esquire class of England in the 1660s, according to Dennis's testimony, it is in part because they are more fully developed than the personages of Etherege's first play. Instead of the twenty-five individualized characters of all classes plus the rout of attendants that are found in *The Comical Revenge,* there are now but thirteen, plus attendants. Instead of the four plots in twenty-six scenes, a prologue, and three epilogues in *The Comical Revenge,* there are three tightly connected plots in ten scenes in *She Would If She Could.* The essence of the action is the inexorable taming of two good-hearted but predatory gentleman wits, despite the tempting snares cast by two aging would-be rakes and by a sexually insatiable lady. The taming, performed by two sisters of wit, wealth, and beauty, once again puts Etherege on the side of society and the institution of marriage.

As a counterpoint to the healthy chasing of the four young people is the hypocritical plotting of Lady Cockwood, so named for her appetite for sexual congress. And a minor theme is the noisy caterwauling of the impotent Sir Oliver Cockwood, named to indicate his inadequacy as a lover, and the bluff and fun-loving Sir Joslin Jolly. But all three plots are highly dependent upon one another and indeed are woven into a virtual single loose plot: the six main characters in Sir Oliver's extended family (including Mrs. Sentry) are in constant close contact, and the two young rakes, pursuing their witty heiresses, can hardly avoid stumbling over one or more of these family members in the wrong place and at the wrong time throughout the course of their pursuit. As might be expected, Etherege relies heavily on coincidences to move his story along, as the following plot synopsis shows, and he also gives to the young women in *She Would If She Could* the final victory, asserting the centrality of marriage, with all of its imperfections.

Plot Summary

Act 1. As Ned Courtall and Frank Freeman plan their next adventures in love, they are interrupted by Mrs. Sentry, gentlewoman to Lady Cockwood. While Freeman is in hiding, Sentry tells Courtall that her mistress, his old acquaintance, has returned to London. Sentry hides in turn as, by coincidence, the lady's marriage-hating husband Sir Oliver invites Courtall to dine. Sir Oliver's friend Sir Joslin Jolly is staying with the Cockwoods and has brought along two pretty kinswomen, both heiresses. When Sir Oliver leaves, Courtall promises Sentry that he will visit Lady Cockwood. With Sentry gone, Courtall assures Freeman that the lady's honor is still intact for she is too affectionate and insatiable to be tolerated. Nevertheless, she might be a means by which they can meet the heiresses. The men go to join Sir Oliver and Sir Joslin.

In the meantime Lady Cockwood's apprehensions are relieved by the news that Courtall will meet her shortly. She also learns of Sir Oliver's plans for debauchery, but when he asks her permission to dine out, she is so eager to have him gone that she feigns complete trust. The two heiresses, Ariana and Gatty, suspect that Lady Cockwood is not as faithful as she pretends, but the sisters' real interest is in entertaining themselves once again in London.

Act 2. In the Mulberry Garden Courtall and Freeman, taking a brief respite from Sir Oliver and Sir Joslin, decide that Freeman will rejoin the two sots while Courtall visits Lady Cockwood. But when Gatty and Ariana pass by masked, the men engage them in witty conversation, concluding with an agreement to meet the following day—if the men will swear to avoid all other women in the interim.

When Courtall arrives, Lady Cockwood pretends great surprise. But in short order she offers herself to him, and only his previous engagement to Sir Oliver and the promise of a meeting with her the next morning enable him to escape. Lady Cockwood's hypocrisy is revealed even more clearly when she berates Sentry for having left her alone with Courtall and when she criticizes Ariana and Gatty for going out alone. The sisters are startled by the arrival of the two drunken knights, who bring along the two young wits from the Mulberry Garden. While Sir Joslin attempts to reconcile the Cockwoods, the young men, recognizing the sisters as the masked women, continue their earlier flirtation, and all agree to meet the following day.

Act 3. The next morning Courtall plots with one of the New Exchange women, Mrs. Gazette, to help him avoid Lady Cockwood by bringing Gatty and Ariana to interrupt them. He invites all three women to "a treat and a fiddle" at the Bear eating-house, but he is embarrassed when his meeting with the girls in the Mulberry Garden is nearly revealed.

The separate threads of the plot now meet at the Bear. Despite his vow to Lady Cockwood to maintain a "day of humiliation" for his conduct the night before, Sir Oliver goes off in his absurd penitential suit to dine with Sir Joslin, Mr. Rakehell, and a bevy of harlots. By coincidence, Courtall, Freeman, and the ladies arrive at the Bear just ahead of them, and Courtall contrives a plan to prevent the discovery of the ladies: they will dress up in masquerade costumes and pretend to be the harlots. In the dance that follows Sir Oliver praises his partner and scorns his wife, not knowing that the woman in his arms is Lady Cockwood. As Sir Oliver grows more aggressive, she pretends to faint, is unmasked by Sentry, and reproaches her husband for his perfidious conduct. Although Sir Oliver feigns penitence, he is ready shortly to follow Sir Joslin to a new appointment with Mrs. Rampant and her harlots.

Act 4. In spite of her temporary triumph over her husband, Lady Cockwood is unhappy at the attentions Courtall has paid to Gatty. In order to test his constancy she forges letters of invitation from the girls to the men so that Courtall must choose between her and Gatty. When Courtall responds that urgent business must keep him from her, Lady Cockwood knows that the business is Gatty, and in a jealous rage tells Sir Oliver that Courtall has tried to seduce her. She easily talks him out of dueling with Courtall, but Sir Oliver still goes off to join Sir Joslin and the harlots. In order to turn Gatty against Courtall, Lady Cockwood then tells the girls that Courtall has bragged that the girls will meet the men anywhere. Her jealousy is heightened when Ariana reveals that the sisters had met the men the night before in the Mulberry Garden, at the very time she was waiting for Courtall.

In the meantime, because the harlots have refused to waste any more time with them, the two knights decide to spend the rest of the evening in drinking and gambling. Not knowing Sir Oliver is nearby, Courtall and Freeman arrive at the New Spring Garden in response to the notes supposedly written by Gatty and Ariana. When Courtall explains that he has luckily escaped Lady Cockwood, Freeman warns him that he himself is now interested in her.

Quite coincidentally, the two girls arrive in the New Spring Garden. When they charge the men with boasting of their familiarity with them, Freeman protests that he and Courtall have the sisters' letters of invitation. At Lady Cockwood's sudden entrance Courtall and Freeman suspect that she is somehow involved. Her attempt to charge the men with counterfeiting the letters as a form of blackmail, however, is nearly exposed when Sentry reveals secretly to her that Gatty can recognize Sentry's handwriting. Just in time Sir Oliver enters, attacks Courtall, and the two fight off the stage with the ladies shrieking and following.

Act 5. Lady Cockwood has sent word to Freeman to visit her, both in hopes of regaining the letters and because she finds she likes him. Just as she is assuring him that the letters were sent by a friend, Courtall arrives and Freeman is hurried into a closet. Courtall's efforts to discover the cause of Sir Oliver's violent hatred, however, are interrupted when the man himself arrives and Lady Cockwood must hide Courtall under a table. A rapid series of farcical events then follows: Sir Oliver bends to pick up an orange; to prevent his seeing Courtall, Sentry rushes the candle away; Sir Oliver chases after her; Lady Cockwood thrusts Courtall into the closet with Freeman, and Sir Oliver returns, followed by Ariana and Gatty. Complaining that she is still upset at the near-duel, Lady Cockwood takes Sir Oliver away, Sentry with them, and Gatty and Ariana promise to leave promptly.

Without knowing that the two men are listening, the sisters discuss their fondness for them and their suspicion that Lady Cockwood was responsible for the letters and is in love with Courtall. But when Ariana discovers the men, the sisters' shrieks bring the Cockwoods back into the room. With a display of quick wit, Courtall blames Sentry for their being in the room, explaining that they had bribed her to hide them in order to learn if the "letters" episode had ruined their friendship with the girls. Lady Cockwood, of course, is pleased at Courtall's cleverness and in turn explains to Sir Oliver that she now knows Courtall's advances to her to have been merely his "French breeding." And when the sisters discover Sentry's hand in the letters, Courtall says it was Lady Cockwood's device to scare them out of going out unchaperoned. Lady Cockwood returns the favor by assuring Gatty that her story of Courtall's boast to Mrs. Gazette was also contrived as a part of her plot to tame the girls. Gatty and Ariana in turn warn that, in case the two men had been guilty of forgery, the girls would have counterfeited wedding contracts to embarrass them.

This disclosure leads to a brief wit-combat on marriage and then to a rapid series of events that leave no strand of the knot untied: Sir Joslin enters with Rakehell but is prevailed upon by Sir Oliver to send the harlots away; Courtall and Freeman concur in their dismissal since they now have a mind to matrimony, and they extract, with Sir Joslin's permission, the sisters' agreement to a month-long courtship. Lady Cockwood forgives Sir Joslin, restores Sentry to her good graces, explains to Courtall that Freeman's visit was her effort to reconcile Courtall and Sir Oliver, and concludes with a vow to confine herself henceforth to family matters. Sir Joslin promises the young people an early marriage, and Sir Oliver brings all to a close with a pledge of love to his lady.

Pretty Heiresses and Witty Rakes

The story of *She Would If She Could* belongs more to the two heiresses Gatty and Ariana than it does to either of the other two pairs of characters or to the solitary Lady Cockwood. Charlene M. Taylor, in her edition of the play,[6] rightly says that Etherege's most significant innovation in the typical love chase plot of Restoration comedy is the use of these two single, emancipated women. Etherege gives to the young women the mastery over nearly every scene in which they appear, through a combination of their good looks, liveliness, wit, and common sense. The fact that the Jolly sisters are also mistresses of their own estates, those pretty countryseats that Courtall considers to be a prerequisite to marriage, gives them added strength as characters, a degree of independence that rescues them from the dominance of their kinsman Sir Joslin Jolly and their more distant relatives the Cockwoods and that frees them from the necessity of making hasty choices of marriage partners.

The great appeal of Ariana and Gatty rests in their clear-eyed view of the world as it is and the people in it as they are. Young men are a necessary albeit sometimes appealing evil, although the girls envy the men's independence almost to the point of foolish imitation. "I do hope you do not intend we shall play such mad reaks as we did last summer," says Ariana to Getty. But of course Gatty does intend. "How I envy that sex!" she exclaims. "We cannot plague 'em enough when we have it in our power for those privileges which custom has allowed 'em above us." Ariana agrees: "The truth is, they can run and ramble here, and there, and everywhere, and we poor fools rather think the better of 'em." In the courtship game that the girls play with Courtall and Freeman, almost every speech contains a pointed criticism of the frailty of the male sex: men are "perjured, perfidious, inconstant, ingrateful," says Gatty; and they are insufferably vain and impudent to boot. The vehemence with which these sentiments are uttered is called for by the game being played, for the men do possess compensating qualities, enough to make the game interesting.

With Lady Cockwood and Sir Oliver the two girls are equally perceptive, but they have no stake in the affairs of those two fops, except as examples of bad marital conduct and as a source of private delight at the opportunities the Cockwood household provides for making titillating discoveries. Hence, the girls' observations are more offhand and understated, often spoken as asides. Almost the first speech by Gatty (1.2) expresses her pleased suspicion that Lady Cockwood is carrying on an affair: "My dear Ariana," she concludes, "how glad am I we are in this town again." And Ariana, when Lady Cockwood learns that her husband has just arrived at the Bear, sums up the essence of her relative's character in a crisp phrase: "Now shall we have admirable sport, what with her fear and jealousy" (3.3). Lady Cockwood's fear is that she will be discovered in Courtall's company; her jealousy is for Sir Oliver's consorting with "a fresh girl or two" when he can scarcely pay his marriage debt (as the wife of Bath would say) at home. About Sir Oliver the two sisters say even less, but one remark by Gatty, the wittier girl of the two, is as profoundly revealing of character as any bon mot penned by Etherege. They are observing the fulsomely penitent Sir Oliver as he pleads for Lady Cockwood's forgiveness at the Bear. "I dare say he counterfeited his sin," says Gatty, "and is real in his repentance" (3.3). That insight is of a man whose compulsion is to appear to the world a rake and to his wife an affectionate husband but who has the capacity for neither role and whose life is indeed perpetual repentance.

In an age in which marriages were arranged by parents in order to benefit the holdings of each family in land and other property, the Jolly sisters are unusually free in their ability to choose husbands according to their own desires. The degree of control exerted over them in London by their relatives is slight, although Sir Joslin Jolly, perhaps their uncle, has sufficient authority to promise them in marriage to Courtall and Freeman. Presumably the girls are now parentless, but their upbringing has prepared them to survive on their own. While they believe in maintaining their honor as much as Lady Cockwood does in maintaining hers, they also recognize that little risked is little gained. Hence, they enter enthusiastically into the love-game with the two young men, but with a clear objective in mind. In the battle of the sexes, which they understand very well, the goal is to attract the men by means of their beauty, wit, and wealth but to preserve their virginity until the men have been reduced to "servants," that is, to courtly lovers who dote on their mistresses and will do anything for them, including marry them. It is a pattern that prevails, as Professor Wilkinson points out, in the comedies of Charles II's reign, a pattern that suggests "something like the triumph of order in a world of comic anarchy."[7]

While the two young heiresses have come to London with the clear intention of snaring husbands, the two young heroes have no such expressed ambitions. Their libertine nature is evident as early as their names—as Dale Underwood has noted[8]—and the opening scene in *She Would If She Could* finds them committed to nothing more in life than repeating the boring routine of eating, drinking, and consorting with the same old female acquaintances. The possibility of fresh amours lures them into the flirtation in the Mulberry Garden with the two masked women, but not until the men discover that these are the heiresses mentioned by Sentry do they begin to consider that marriage might result. When the young wits meet in the New Exchange the next morning, that inclination begins to be revealed. Courtall tells Freeman that women deliberately seek out the rakish man: " 'Tis a sign of youth and high mettle, and makes them rather *piqué,* who shall tame him." Freeman's response suggests that his hope is for more than a brief affair: "If we are anything fortunate in our contrivance, we shall make it a pleasant comedy" (3.1). In one sense of the word, a comedy is a story with a happy ending, and while Freeman may hope for more, no happy ending short of marriage is likely for a pair of heiresses of wit and beauty.

The mutual pursuit of the belles and beaux in *She Would If She Could* is carried on in witty language that is often drawn from the vocabulary of trade, the hunt, rural sports, war, and—as noted earlier—law. In exploiting for comic effect the gap between appearance and reality, Etherege has his young wits speak in act 1 of their love affairs as "the old trade," of pimps as "civil officers," of prostitutes as part of the "markets," where there are "purveyors" engaged in "trade and industry." Even when the two men talk about meeting the heiresses mentioned by Sentry, Freeman speaks of the hoped-for flirtation as playing a while "upon tick" (credit), and Courtall hopes for "payment hereafter," a neat pun on sexual success as well as on the gaining of an estate by means of marriage. In 2.1, when the young men enter the Mulberry Garden just before meeting the girls, Courtall rebukes Freeman for acting as if the men were "upon a hot scent," and Freeman speaks of the impending visit to Lady Cockwood's as "start[ing] the game." They continue in that same spirit when the masked girls appear, referring to them as "country fillies," with experience in running sports like "course-a-park" and "barley-break."

The girls in their turn liken the wits to men-of-war "cruising here, to watch for prizes," who—if valiant—will "make more sail and board us." And so it goes throughout the courtship until the end of the play, when the metaphoric language of trade merges into the real language of marriage contracts in this exchange:

> GATTY. The truth is, such experienced gentlemen as you are, seldom mortgage your persons without it be to redeem your estates.
>
> COURTALL. 'Tis a mercy we have scaped the mischief so long, and are likely to do penance only for our own sins; most families are a wedding behind-hand in the world, which makes so many young men fooled into wives, to pay their fathers' debts: all the happiness a gentleman can desire, is to live at liberty, till he be forced that way to pay his own. (5.1)

There is more here than mere wit, although that is laugh-provoking enough. Gatty is offering the challenge to Courtall: "Are you interested in marrying me only for my money?" Courtall is responding: "I'm a man of independent means and not a fortune hunter seeking to pay off the family debt." One more exchange, still in the language of trade, seals their agreement:

> GATTY. These gentlemen have found it so convenient lying in lodgings, they'll hardly venture on the trouble of taking a house of their own.
>
> COURTALL. A pretty country-seat, madam, with a handsome parcel of land, and other necessaries belonging to't, may tempt us; but for a town-tenement that has but one poor conveniency, we are resolved we'll never deal. (5.1)

Gatty is asking: "Are you sure you can be satisfied with a single wife when you have had such a variety of mistresses?" Courtall's response continues her metaphor: "A charming country wife is far preferable to the town women we've known; we'd never settle for them." But at the same time, his metaphor of the pretty countryseat affirms his requirement that the woman for him must bring to marriage a respectable fortune.

Both the men and the women of the love-game have reached the threshold of an agreement that the audience can only applaud. They are matched in wit and attractiveness, their estates will likely prove to be compatible, and—best of all—they have found one another freely, rather than having been forced into arranged marriages. As the audience can see, only happiness can ensue, if the two couples can survive the month-long engagement that they agree upon in the final minutes of act 5.

Sir Oliver Cockwood and Sir Joslin Jolly

As if to warn the belles and beaux that carelessness in courtship can have dire results, Etherege offers the foolish Cockwoods and Sir Joslin Jolly as examples of wrong conduct in the relationship between the sexes. Sir Joslin is the most nearly innocent of the three fools, to be sure, and—but for his pursuit of whores—is a kind of Sir Roger de Coverley in his good-hearted enjoyment of simple pleasures. Jocelyn Powell considers him to be directly related to Sir Frederick Frollick in *The Comical Revenge,* with all of that rake's animal spirits and his delight in music, song, and dance.[9] And so he is. But he is Sir Frederick grown old and without a wife, perhaps because, as he says to Cockwood, "man and wife are seldom in good humour alone" (2.2). His many songs are his special expression of his exuberance, and Etherege uses them at key points, often to underscore personality traits and plot developments. Sir John's first song, for example, sketches the character of each of the heiresses, helping further to distinguish one from the other:

> This is sly and pretty,
> And this is wild and witty;
> If either stayed
> Till she died a maid,
> I'faith 'twould be great pity. (2.2)

In the last act, just as the two young couples are coming to an agreement to marry, Sir Joslin enters with a song that advocates open enjoyment of the good things of life. He concludes: "Hang your temperate sot, / Who would seem what he's not; / 'Tis I am wise, he's but grave." It is frank advice, if they will take it, to the young people, who have yet to admit openly their desires to one another. In a moment they do, the men vowing themselves "humble servants" and the women accepting them.

Frank and good-natured as he is, Sir Joslin Jolly stands in sharp contrast to Sir Oliver Cockwood. While the uncomplicated Sir Joslin confesses his desires openly and seeks to satisfy them in the same way, Sir Oliver has created two opposing personas for himself and lives uneasily between them. As a would-be libertine his pose is absurd to the extreme in its reduction of love to its lowest animal level. In his first meeting with Courtall he suggests sexual activities so casual and careless that the rakish talk of the young men sounds refined: "If one chance but to couple himself with his neighbour's daughter," Sir Oliver says, "without the help of the parson of the parish, and leave a little testimony of his kindness behind him, there is presently such an uproar, that a poor man is fain to fly his country: . . ." It is clear from Lady Cockwood's later speeches, however, that Sir Oliver is virtually impotent and so his "talk of strange matters" (2.1), as she puts it, is mere pretense. "He is not able to play the spark abroad thus, I assure you," she tells Sentry, and speaks scornfully of "that poor stock of comfort I should have at home" (3.3).

At the other extreme of Sir Oliver's pretense is his professed affection for and loyalty to his wife, at the very time he is attempting to conceal his libertine aspirations from her. What the audience finds especially funny is his further folly in believing that his wife is the epitome of chaste behavior. The comic high point of their mutual hypocrisy comes in the scene at the Bear (3.3), when Sir Oliver, thinking he is dancing with a prostitute, is in reality dancing with his own wife. When he refers to Lady Cockwood with contempt as "that domestic instrument of mine" and then offers to attack briskly the woman at his side (his wife in disguise), she pretends to faint and is revealed for who she is, Lady Cockwood. The confusion of the scene is delicious and must have brought the biggest laughs from the audience. Jacob Tonson thought so, and a generation later included the scene as the frontispiece to the comedy in his 1715 edition of *The Works*. In the melee that follows Sir Oliver exhibits what seems for a time to be a real repentance, and Lady Cockwood—to the disgust of Courtall—rebukes her husband for perfidious conduct while holding herself up as a paragon of wifely loyalty. But Sir Oliver relapses quickly and by the end of the scene has recovered his hypocritical nature and is ready for a romp later on with Madam Rampant and her whores.

Lady Cockwood

In naming his comedy *She Would If She Could* Etherege called attention to the most intriguing of the personages, Lady Cockwood. Over a century ago Edmund Gosse concluded that she was a character of such complexity that Etherege must have borrowed her outline from Molière's Tartuffe. Indeed, Gosse felt so certain that Lady Cockwood was "founded upon a reminiscence of Tartuffe" that he imagined Etherege to have been present at the 1664 or 1667 performance, inasmuch as the French play was not printed until 1669.[10] While it is quite possible that Etherege was in Paris in one of these years and possible even that he had seen *Tartuffe,* it was not necessary for him to have known that play in order to fashion the comparatively simple personality of Lady Cockwood, who has neither the malice nor the sophistication of Molière's villain. As a matter of fact, Etherege might have found her type in earlier English plays by James Shirley and Thomas Killigrew, as has been suggested,[11] or he could have created her out of whole cloth, as a type well known in English society.

Lady Cockwood draws our interest for a number of reasons, beginning with our curiosity about a woman of wealth and beauty who must seek sexual gratification outside marriage. Moreover, those affairs must be conducted—if she is to maintain her sense of honor—according to the code of précieuse courtship. And finally, she impresses us with her sheer energy: she sends word instantly to Courtall, waits impatiently for him, urges an assignation, dances in disguise at the Bear and counterfeits a fit, indulges in passionate outbursts, and throughout the comedy simply dominates Sir Oliver, holding his penitential suit *in terrorem* as a means of reproving his excesses and freeing her for her own.

That she is a handsome woman is clear from the young men's and Sir Oliver's comments about her, and that fact piques an audience's curiosity to know why she should seek amours so avidly away from home. Although a number of scholars have assumed that her charms are faded or that her "physical equipment is not of the best,"[12] Courtall speaks of her "rare beauty" (1.1), and Sir Oliver—not seeing through her disguise at the Bear—announces with delight, "What a shape is here, Ned! so exact and tempting, . . ." (3.3). The fact that witty young rakes like Courtall and Freeman would condescend to consider an affair with her further confirms that she is physically attractive.

One important key to Lady Cockwood's conduct, certainly, is the sexual passion she is not able to fulfill at home. That she is intended to be laughed at for her lust is clear from Etherege's treatment of her in the play and from the fact that she is an early example of the sex-starved women who are ridiculed in the plays and poetry of the period. Etherege's own Loveit in *The Man of Mode* is a descendant of Lady Cockwood, and Congreve's Lady Wishfort in *The Way of the World* is the best-known character of the type. In a study of women in Restoration satiric poetry, Reba Wilkinson argues that the topic of the insatiable woman is so prominent "that it takes on the character of an obsession."[13] Because of Sir Oliver's impotence, however, Lady Cockwood's frustration is understandable; and were it not for the absurdity of her social pretenses and précieuse posing, she would be a sympathetic character, even in an age that seems to have believed in women's "natural coldness," as Congreve put it.[14]

When Courtall first describes Lady Cockwood to Freeman, he characterizes her as "the very spirit of impertinence, so foolishly fond and troublesome that no man above sixteen is able to endure her." What he means specifically is that the lady is living in a dream world of *préciosité* in which there are those heroic men and those ladies of divine beauty who can win them with their ocular powers. Were there no more to her folly than this, she would have been laughable as a parody of the noble ladies of the type of the upper plot in *The Comical Revenge*. Her perpetual expressions of concern for her honor, her fainting spells, her melodramatic outbursts, and her threat to retire to the country—all of these are marks of the précieuse. As David Berkeley points out, however, the true précieuse was unable to translate her desire into action: "Thus Restoration theater-goers were prepared to savor Lady Cockwood's ranting about 'honour' . . . for she was not merely a decayed pretender to virtue . . . but a false précieuse."[15] A single exchange between Lady Cockwood and Courtall sums up the paradox of her sexual lust and her précieuse pose:

> COURTALL. . . . my concern for your honour will make me so feverish and disordered, that I shall lose the taste of all the happiness you give me.
>
> LADY COCKWOOD. Methinks you are too scrupulous, heroic sir. (3.1)

The comedy lies in that "heroic sir," an epithet worthy of the court of Queen Henrietta Maria, but bestowed on a man with whom Lady Cockwood intends to have sexual intercourse.

At the end of the play it is clear that the Cockwoods will be returning to their farm home, where Lady Cockwood will be doomed once more to that "sad time in the country" that Sentry had complained of to Courtall. Very likely Lady Cockwood did not catch the meaning of Courtall's response to her act 5 avowal to "confine myself to the humble affairs of my own family." That response was "'Tis a very pious resolution, madam, and the better to confirm you in it, pray entertain an able chaplain." An affair with a chaplain would be an unlikely compromise for her, lacking that aura of honor that could turn affairs into adventures. Rightly she blames fortune for her dilemma, for it could not have been the design of the Cockwoods to be so entirely incompatible in marriage. Although the ending of the comedy is thus ironic for them, for the young people there is a degree of hope. Rather than accepting the men blindly, the young women insist on "a month's experience of your good behavior"; and the men are aware that it will be a period of testing, for Courtall knows that the heart of man can be deceitful, and Freeman knows that "a month is a tedious time."

Chapter Four

The Man of Mode; or, Sir Fopling Flutter (1676)

"'Tis an Old Mistress"

George Etherege's third and last comedy was written and produced when he was forty years old—an "old mistress," in Sir Car Scroope's "Prologue" to the play—and the men who acted the leading parts were all middle-aged. Thomas Betterton, who had the all-important role of Dorimant in *The Man of Mode,* was forty-one; Henry Harris, who portrayed Medley, was forty-two, having inaugurated the role of Sir Frederick Frollick a dozen years earlier in *The Comical Revenge;* and William Smith, who played Sir Fopling Flutter, was also in middle age. He had created the role of the dashing Colonel Bruce in Etherege's first play. The selection of these aging actors to portray the cynical rakes of *The Man of Mode* may well have appeared appropriate to the audience in 1676, and the world-weary tone of the dialogue in much of the play has impressed readers ever since. Even Sir Fopling Flutter's silly capering takes on a note of seriousness when the role is played by an actor in his forties rather than one in his twenties. The characer of Dorimant, especially in those scenes in which his antisocial, destructive qualities are most strongly expressed, and when played by an actor in middle age, must of necessity seem more closely allied to the ill-natured old bachelor types of humors comedy than to young wits like the lighthearted lovers of Etherege's own *She Would If She Could.* Indeed—except for the ill nature—Dorimant appears to be very like what Etherege himself was at this latter stage of his life: witty, proud, and predatory.

From its first performance in 1676 to the present *The Man of Mode* has been Etherege's most controversial as well as his most popular play. If it has been performed rarely since the seventeenth century, it has been included in numerous anthologies in the twentieth century and has also been separately reprinted several times. What has given it the degree of popularity it enjoyed with seventeenth-century audiences and now enjoys among twentieth-century readers continues to be a challenge for scholarship. Is it the interest in troublesome questions of the individual versus society that are raised by the comedy—and left unanswered? Is it fascination with the attractive-repellent personality of Dorimant, or with that of the irritating-appealing Sir Fopling Flutter, or with that of the arrogant-beautiful Harriet? No contemporary reactions to the play have come down to us from Etherege's time, except the most general statements, comments like Charles Gildon's "extraordinary" and Downes's "got a great deal of money." Convincing and precise information about the audience's response is, as John Barnard has put it, "at best incomplete, at worst conjectural."[1] Even interpretations by contemporary readers who are well informed about the society of the time and about the drama that appealed to that society are frequently in disagreement.

The most convincing recent examination of the audience for whom George Etherege intended *The Man of Mode* is that by John Barnard.[2] For him the challenge in reading *The Man of Mode* is to determine how a very popular play in a public theater, with an audience made up of widely diverse members of society, could create a sympathetic attitude in that audience "very close to the sceptical and aggressive irreverence of Dorimant."[3] In order to make such a determination, Barnard finds a variety of clues that, upon interpretation, give a detailed picture of the specific audience that was intended in 1676 and how its members were supposed to react.

That the comedy was meant principally for a court-related audience is evidenced in a number of ways. Barnard points out that the entire court attended *The Man of Mode* at its opening and several times thereafter and that the maids of honor are recorded as having gone to the play on at least one occasion. Moreover, Etherege intentionally employs a rich mixture of literary and historical references that could be understood only by an audience made up principally of courtiers. Among the examples Barnard offers of such references two are of particular interest: allusions in the comedy to current London opera productions and to contemporary French literature. The opera references are to Thomas Shadwell's *Psyche* and *The Tempest,* both performed during the 1675–76 season and on the very stage where *The Man of Mode* was being acted and for the same audience. In act 1 of *The Man of Mode* the whore Molly asks Dorimant for "a guynie to see the operies," and he sends it to her so that she can "perk up i' the face of quality." Only an audience that knew these operas would catch the joke, says Barnard, and only those within it who could side with Dorimant and Medley would laugh at the idea of a whore in the most expensive seats, "perking up" amid quality. A few lines later Dorimant exits, singing a few lines from Shadwell's *The Tempest,* an opera about the love of two innocents and hence, Barnard suggests, a satiric comment, which some in the audience would understand, on the sentimental taste of Molly.

A second clue to the sophistication of the audience that Etherege wrote to please is found by Professor Barnard in the exchange between Harriet and Sir Fopling Flutter relating to the scandalous *Histoire amoureuse des Gaulles*. The joke on Sir Fopling, who confuses the French author, the Compte de Bussy, with a character created by the English playwright George Chapman, assumes not only that the young men and women of *The Man of Mode* have read Bussy's book in French but that a large segment of the audience has done so also. Hence the wits and courtiers are expected by Etherege to know precisely how Sir Fopling's phony French sophistication differs from their own presumably true sophistication. It is their awareness of the distinction between the true and false men of mode, as Barnard rightly points out, that is an important source of the comedy of the play.

The assumption that Etherege intended his comedy to please a sophisticated, court-related coterie is helpful to an understanding of the effect of the comedy, and Professor Barnard goes on to suggest ways in which the playwright sought to win over to the side of Dorimant and the wits the less educated members of the audience. Nevertheless, the range of response to *The Man of Mode* by readers over the centuries promises that the comedy will always be controversial. Like *Hamlet,* Etherege's masterpiece will continue to have as many interpretations as there are schools of criticism and individual readers. The summary of critical perspectives in David Mann's recent reference guide to Etherege[4] is a useful introduction to the wide range of attitudes toward individuals in the play and toward the plot, the resolution of which has tended to make most readers uneasy.

Plot Summary

In the following synopsis of *The Man of Mode* much of the basis for that audience unease can be seen, as well as the basis for understanding the complex characters who comprise the story.

Act 1. At the very time that Dorimant has determined to break with his jealous mistress Loveit, he learns from Nan the Orange Woman that a spirited young gentlewoman has fallen in love with him. From his friend Medley he discovers further that she is an heiress named Harriet Woodvill, lately come to town with her mother. Medley's description of her beauty and wit make Dorimant eager to meet her. In the meantime Dorimant has hatched a plot with his new love, Bellinda, to make Loveit so madly jealous that she will initiate the break. This plot takes on added complexity when, having learned that Sir Fopling Flutter is back from France, Dorimant determines to bring him and Loveit together in order to charge her with fondness for a fool.

A decided contrast to the profligate Dorimant is his lovesick friend Young Bellair, desperate to marry the modest Emilia but frustrated by the designs of his father, who plans to marry his son elsewhere. By coincidence, old Bellair has taken rooms in the same house where Emilia lives, not knowing she loves his son.

Act 2. Emilia and her friend Lady Townley have managed to keep young Bellair's love for Emilia a secret, but now the father has fallen into a foolish passion for Emilia and is threatening to marry her himself in order to disinherit his disobedient son. The girl Old Bellair has chosen for his son is Harriet, the heiress who admires Dorimant. While father and son Bellair are off visiting the Woodvills, Medley entertains Lady Townley and Emilia with the story of Loveit's violent jealousy of Dorimant.

In the next scene that jealousy is displayed. Although she wants to believe the excuse that Dorimant sends for avoiding her, Mrs. Loveit is aroused by her servant Pert, who charges Dorimant with ridiculing his mistress behind her back, and then by Bellinda, who reports that she saw him at the play the night before with a masked woman. When Dorimant arrives, he defends himself against Loveit's charge of inconstancy by pleading that he is too young for a permanent relationship, and he accuses her in turn of encouraging Sir Fopling's attentions. While Bellinda has done her part in Dorimant's scheme to break off with Loveit, she is sobered by Loveit's violence and Dorimant's skilled dissembling.

Act 3. At Lady Woodvill's, Harriet's irritation at Busy's officious hairdressing reveals that her dislike of affectation matches Dorimant's; but Busy says that Harriet is annoyed because she is fonder of Dorimant than of Bellair, whom her mother has selected for her.

In order to buy time, Young Bellair and Harriet pretend to be courting, and so please their parents.

While Young Bellair is at Lady Woodvill's, Bellinda arrives at Lady Townley's to entertain Emilia and Lady Townley further with the story of Loveit's jealousy. Dorimant joins them and in secret makes a rendezvous with Bellinda for the following morning. At this moment occurs the long-awaited arrival of Sir Fopling Flutter. After a tour de force of foppery, in which he admires Emilia's lace, praises Medley as a critic of clothes, and discusses with the group the fine points of his own ensemble, Sir Fopling reveals to Dorimant his interest in Loveit. Dorimant is pleased at this opportunity to advance his plot and promises Fopling that he can meet Loveit that night in the Mall.

That evening Bellair and Harriet walk in the Mall, talking of Dorimant, whose reputation has thrown Lady Woodvill into an agony of apprehension. Dorimant now introduces himself, but his brief wit-combat with Harriet is interrupted by Lady Woodvill, who comes to take her daughter away from the dangers of the Mall. Although she does not know what Dorimant looks like, she hears Sir Fopling call his name at a distance, and, startled that he should be somewhere about, hurries away with Harriet.

Sir Fopling's arrival turns Dorimant's attention to his plan to break with Loveit. Loveit in turn has vowed to Bellinda that she will make Dorimant jealous, and her attentions to Sir Fopling do exactly that. Medley's laughter increases Dorimant's embarrassment, and he vows to be revenged on Loveit. The two men go off to join Bellair and the Woodvills for dancing at Lady Townley's, where Dorimant is to pretend to be Mr. Courtage.

Act 4. At Lady Townley's, to the amusement of the rest of the company, "Courtage" has been charming Lady Woodvill. Old Bellair, in turn, has been proposing himself as a husband to Emilia. At his first opportunity Dorimant rebukes Harriet for her coldness but finds himself more deeply in love than ever before. They are interrupted by the arrival of Sir Fopling, to talk of his intrigues in Paris, his flirtations at court, and his past skill at dancing. When she sees Fopling, however, Lady Woodvill once again rushes Harriet away for she fears Dorimant is in his company. Dorimant in turn hastens off to meet Bellinda. After drinking with Old Bellair, Fopling leads Medley and Bellair off to awaken Dorimant.

Meantime, having just made love with Dorimant, Bellinda extracts from him his vow never to see Loveit again; but her departure is hastened by the arrival of Fopling and company. Dorimant learns that Bellair is shortly to be married, and Bellair warns him that matrimony is the only way to gain Harriet. If he marries her, Dorimant observes, he will obtain a good estate as well. First, however, he must have his revenge on Loveit.

Having escaped Dorimant's without being seen, Bellinda is taken by mistake to Loveit's house.

Act 5. Although Bellinda manages to quiet Loveit's suspicions of her early morning arrival, the news of Dorimant's sudden coming is so great a shock that Pert must lead Bellinda off to lie down. Dorimant maliciously pretends to believe that Loveit is fond of Sir Fopling, and after a bitter quarrel with her, declares that he will consider his reputation cleared only if she will ridicule Sir Fopling that night. She refuses, and Bellinda joins her to abuse Dorimant. After his embarrassed departure and Loveit's promise to pursue him in order to discover his new lover, Bellinda vows never to risk herself in such an affair again.

At Lady Townley's we learn that young Bellair and Emilia are now secretly married. Emilia tries to lead Harriet to admit that she is in love with Dorimant, but only Dorimant himself, arriving suddenly from Loveit's, can bring her close to confessing her love. When old Bellair orders Parson Smirk to marry his son and Harriet, Smirk announces that he has already married Young Bellair. Old Bellair receives a second shock when he attempts to marry Emilia in order to disinherit his son, for he discovers that she is Young Bellair's bride.

In the general consternation that ensues Loveit and Bellinda arrive, having followed Dorimant to Lady Townley's. Lady Woodvill learns that Courtage is in reality Dorimant and tries to take Harriet away, but the daughter refuses to go. Dorimant secretly chides Loveit for almost spoiling his chance at obtaining an estate, suggesting that they might even have continued as lovers. Bellinda, however, rejects his attempt to explain his deceit to her and refuses to meet him again. The efforts of Harriet, Medley, and Lady Townley, meantime, to change Lady Woodvill's opinion of Dorimant, have brought her to agree reluctantly to his courtship of Harriet; and Medley further extracts from Old Bellair his blessing on Young Bellair and Emilia.

All that is needed now is Sir Fopling. His arrival and Harriet's jeers drive Loveit from the scene. Harriet agrees to permit Dorimant to court her in the country, and Old Bellair calls for a dance, to end the play.

Dorimant

To the same degree that Sir Frederick Frollick dominates *The Comical Revenge,* so Dorimant dominates *The Man of Mode.* Both men are in control of their limited worlds, each lives for pleasure until a woman of wit and wealth succeeds in taming him, and each defines in his person and behavior Etherege's view of the true man of mode at a particular point in the development of English society. The principal difference between the two is the degree to which each is a healing or a destructive ingredient in that society, and in this competition Sir Frederick wins out as the mender of social ills. It is fortunate for society that it has such iron-willed beauties as Harriet to bring the Dorimants of the world to heel. And how she accomplishes that feat and how convincing the conversion might have appeared to a sophisticated court audience are the principal questions of the play. If Dorimant takes a step or two in the last act toward reformation, in particular in his conciliatory conduct toward Mrs. Loveit and Bellinda and in his willingness to live away from his beloved London, it is in large measure because he has a new respect for the power of love that motivated those two passionate women; he is now significantly under its power himself. But there are other elements too that contribute to his near-reformation.

The first view of Dorimant in the opening scene of *The Man of Mode* gives little hint that this man of arrogance and affectation is likely to capitulate to any woman. His soliloquy, prefaced with the reciting of two lines from Edmund Waller's heroic poem "Of a War With Spain, and Fight at Sea," is a bored complaint about the difficulty of shedding an old mistress. It is followed by a series of witty but brutal exchanges among Dorimant, his servants, the Orange Woman, and the Shoemaker, concluding in conversation with Medley and Young Bellair that completes the first-act exposition needed to advance the action of the comedy.

With his servants Dorimant is on an ambivalent footing, for the brisk repartee between him and Handy and the footman illustrates both the rigidity of the hierarchical social structure of seventeenth-century London and the deviations from it that produce laughter as well as egalitarian applause. Dorimant's efforts to exert control over his manservant Handy are frustrated with the first order given:

DORIMANT. Call a footman.

HANDY. None of 'em are come yet.

DORIMANT. Dogs! will they ever lie snoring abed till noon.

HANDY. 'Tis all one, sir: if they're up, you indulge 'em so, they're ever poaching after whores all the morning. (1.1)

Not only does Handy not produce the servant required but he rebukes his master for his indulgent mismanagement of his household staff.

Harsh as Dorimant is in speaking to his servants, his bark is much worse than his bite. At the end of act 1, when Dorimant calls Handy "blockhead" and "sot," the servant responds with an impudent "Did you call me, sir?" It is a fine exchange, exaggerated slightly for Medley's benefit, but clearly revealing of two men of different classes, conducting their business with half-humorous raillery, and bound together by wit and especially by necessity: Handy needs his pay and Dorimant needs a loyal and discreet servant, as act 4, scene 2 demonstrates. With the footman, however, one of the loafers described by Handy, Dorimant is severe, and when, at the end of the scene, the servant presumes to suggest a coach instead of waiting for his master's order, Dorimant checks him sarcastically: "I may ride the elephant if I please, sir; call another chair, and let my coach follow to Long's." Whatever the footman may have intended, Dorimant will travel according to his own wishes.

With the Orange Woman and Tom the Shoemaker, Dorimant is on a similarly ambivalent footing. Like his servants, they are a necessary and intimate part of his comfortable existence, but they are also grotesques who invite his mocking scorn. The coterie of court-related wits who made up a part of the audience at *The Man of Mode* would have laughed with Dorimant at the grossly fat Orange Woman with her load of gossip, and the rest of the audience would have laughed at her impudent replies: about Dorimant, "I never knew you to commend anything"; about Medley, "there is not such another heathen in town," a "foul-mouthed rogue." With the entrance of the Shoemaker, "swearing Tom" as Medley calls him, the air rapidly grows thick with insults: Dorimant calls Tom a drunken sot and he responds scornfully that Dorimant has not paid his bills. Medley charges Tom with whoring and swearing, and his answer is that some men of quality, like Dorimant and Medley, deserve the pillory for writing libelous lampoons. The society in which these men live may be a highly stratified one, but Dorimant's fondness for witty conversation and raillery has created an atmosphere of bonhomie that tempers the impression of malice conveyed by his words alone and serves as a faint foreshadowing of his seeming reformation in act 5.

Dorimant and Medley

Early in the opening scene of *The Man of Mode* it appears that Medley is more than a mere companion to the protagonist, convenient for conversation but little else, and it is soon evident also that Dorimant is eager to have his approval. Medley's malice is exhibited early in his exchanges with Nan the Orange Woman and Tom the Shoemaker, and his knowledge of the gossip of London society shows up early as well. He recognizes Lady Woodvill and Harriet immediately from the Orange Woman's outline and fills in details about both, providing that lyrical portrait of Harriet's beauty that later leads Dorimant to exclaim: "You never came so near truth in your life, as you did in her description" (4.3). Medley's powers of observation are great and his fondness for scandal is notorious, especially among the ladies—with whom he is, consequently, very popular. As a result, Dorimant admires him, shows off before him, seeks his approbation but fears his scorn, and in his tricky affair with Loveit wishes nothing higher than Medley's applause for his management of it.

That Medley is much more than a disinterested observer of the London social scene appears in act 1 in his probing into Dorimant's affair with Loveit. "I have had an eye on you," he says, after reading the letter to Loveit. "If some malicious body should betray you, this kind note would hardly make your peace with her." It is Medley's declaration of war, a warfare of the sort that D. R. M. Wilkinson speaks of, in discussing the two men, as "so persistently assumed by the gallants."[5] Dorimant's strategy in this conflict of the wits is to overwhelm Medley with the clever complexity of his devices for getting rid of an old mistress and then—at the appropriate time—with his sudden success in gaining a new one. The strategem, however, may fail, and should it do so, the audience is aware early on that Dorimant is vulnerable to Medley's malice.

The terms that Dale Underwood uses to describe Dorimant's character apply equally well to Medley. Both men exhibit "a Hobbesian aggressiveness, competitiveness, and drive for power and 'glory'; a Machiavellian dissembling and cunning; a satanic pride, vanity, and malice; and drawing upon each of these frames of meaning, an egoistic assertion of self through the control of others."[6] Medley's efforts to control others are exerted with disarming civility: in act 1 he greets Dorimant with fulsome familiarity as "my life, my joy, my darling-sin" and later on is praised by Lady Townley as "a very necessary man among us women; he's not scandalous i' the least, perpetually contriving to bring good company together, and always ready to stop up a gap at ombre, then he knows all the little news o' the town." To this sketch the modest Emilia adds: "I love to hear him talk o' the intrigues, let 'em be never so dull in themselves, he'll make 'em pleasant i' the relation" (2.1). It is Medley's ability to relay gossip, to hold the magnifying glass of exaggeration up to every intrigue, that gives him his power over Dorimant, for Dorimant would die before he would have a failed affair laughed at over ombre or be thought to be seeking a wife for any reason but an estate. As he says to Loveit in their fine quarreling scene (5.1), "Medley, when he is rhetorically drunk, will ever be declaiming on it. . . ." Moreover, Medley is armored in an honest-man invulnerability that Dorimant emulates but cannot achieve because Medley's desires—whether for a mistress, money, or marriage—are so well concealed that he appears to have none. He is a worthy antagonist to the rake-hero of *The Man of Mode*.

At two points in the play Dorimant's vulnerability to Medley's ridicule is most evident: first, when Loveit confounds Dorimant's expectations by appearing to enjoy Sir Fopling's company in the Mall; and second, at the close of act 5, when Loveit and Bellinda arrive at Lady Townley's while Dorimant is pretending to be Mr. Courtage. In both scenes Medley is present, observing and enjoying. In the first of these, in the Mall (3.3), Dorimant's overconfidence invites disaster. "Medley," he says, "you shall see good sport anon between Loveit and this Fopling." And again, "Let us go forward—seem earnest in discourse and show ourselves. Then you shall see how she'll use him." But when Loveit ignores Dorimant and entertains Sir Fopling as if she enjoys his company, Dorimant is dismayed and Medley delighted. "Dorimant," he says, "you look a little bashful on the matter!" And then with deep sarcasm: "Would you had brought some more of your friends, Dorimant, to have been witness of Sir Fopling's disgrace and your triumph." Dorimant's protestations cannot make up for this injury to his pride, and in the scenes that follow, whenever Medley is present, Dorimant is thoroughly on his guard. When Medley comes close to revealing the Bellair-Emilia love affair to Bellair's father, for example, Dorimant warns him: "You'll spoil all with some unseasonable jest, Medley." The liaison with Bellinda he keeps so secret that Medley never learns her name. And, as we have seen, when Dorimant determines to rebuke Loveit for seeming to favor Fopling, he invites Medley to come along as a witness to her humiliation and as a vindication of his own reputation.

It is in act 5, however, that Dorimant is most vulnerable to Medley's critical eye and where he escapes only by the greatest good luck and quick-wittedness. His good luck lies in Loveit's fierce repulse of Sir Fopling Flutter at their final meeting. His quick wit enables him to escape the sort of tirade that Mrs. Loveit levels against Sir Fopling Flutter. Had Dorimant not pacified her as he did, with the explanation that he had broken off with her in order to mend his fortune by means of a marriage to Harriet, he might have had to suffer at least public embarrassment, if not worse, from one of her outbursts. Harriet might have been as angered by Loveit's emotional distress as Bellinda had been earlier, and Dorimant cannot wish that to happen, for his heart is at stake now much more than his fortune. Medley sees only that Loveit has publicly repudiated Sir Fopling (as Dorimant had wished) and that she now accepts that she is a cast mistress—however bitter that acceptance may be. Hence Medley concedes to Dorimant the victory in the genteel contest to see who can better manage the fair sex: "I pronounce thy reputation clear—and henceforward when I would know anything of woman, I will consult no other oracle." Dorimant has won this last skirmish and indeed their brief war, and now can publicly confess his love for Harriet from a position of strength.

Dorimant and Harriet

Probably no other love-combat in the comedies of the later seventeenth century has attracted more interest and resulted in less agreement about its outcome than that between Dorimant and Harriet. Are the two lovers so perfectly matched in wit, wealth, and social position—not to mention their love of inflicting pain—that they will find happiness together in Hampshire and in London? Or is there very little likelihood that a country girl and a city rake can discover a basis for a permanent relationship? Or is it clear, as has often been argued, that Dorimant has no intentions beyond an affair—or a marriage—that will allow him to continue to pursue London mistresses? Or is it impossible to determine what the outcome might be, as Dale Underwood persuasively argues, because the frivolous society in which the lovers live has "no adequate set of values by which that frivolity may be judged"?[7]

How a director might choose to interpret these two characters has a crucial bearing on our perception of the outcome of their love-combat, of course. If *The Man of Mode* is interpreted as a "dark comedy," with Dorimant and Harriet as malicious wits who enjoy inflicting pain and whose pangs of love are seen only as momentary weaknesses, then there is little hope of happiness for them. If the comedy is played with a heavy emphasis on farce—Dorimant nearly as foolish as Sir Fopling and Harriet a whimsical précieuse—then it can be no more than a momentary "exquisite and airy picture of the manners of that age," as William Hazlitt called it in 1819,[8] from which no serious statement can be expected. There are, however, many clues to suggest that neither of these extremes was intended by Etherege, that the audience is meant to laugh less at Dorimant and Harriet than at the fashionable folly of Sir Fopling and the out-of-fashion folly of Old Bellair and Lady Woodvill. Etherege offers the hope that the two lovers, after a long struggle to surmount the précieux artificiality of their society and their own natures, will come to a recognition of the *possibility* at least of happiness with each other.

Harriet and Dorimant belong in many ways to the same heroic world in which Lord Bevill and family had their being in *The Comical Revenge*. At his first meeting with Harriet, for example, near the end of act 3, Dorimant falls into the adoring ecstasy of a heroic lover and is ready at that moment to pursue her with the serious thought of marriage in mind—an idea he has been sneering at until now:

> DORIMANT. [aside] 'Tis she! it must be she, that lovely hair, that easy shape, those wanton eyes, and all those melting charms about her mouth, which Medley spoke of; I'll follow the lottery, and put in for a prize [marriage] with my friend Bellair.

If Dorimant is attracted by Harriet's charms, he does not yet have a high opinion of her intelligence: he expects her, as a précieuse, to require flattery, and he provides it. Only then does he begin to learn that she, in fact, possesses the more than usual amount of wit that Medley had claimed for her in act 1. But Dorimant has a long way to go in his education, if the basis for a lasting relationship is to be something more substantial than that of adoring servant and semidivine lady of beauty and virtue. The audience of the time was aware that whether on the one hand Dorimant might be reduced to a humiliated slave, or on the other might take advantage of the relationship to seduce the lady, the artificial code of Henrietta Maria's Court made equality between the sexes impossible and thus discouraged the development of the friendship between husband and wife that must undergird a successful marriage. At this moment, seeing her for the first time and conversing with her, Dorimant is not concerned that Harriet will disdain him because of his reputation as a seducer of society belles. If Harriet considers herself as a précieuse, as he thinks she does, then she must believe in the power of her love to bring any rake to a reformation. Indeed, so powerfully must that love work that the penitent rake, enslaved by love, will go to any lengths, even to making himself appear ridiculous, to win his mistress's heart. As Harriet puts it at their next meeting, confirming this précieux view of her, "When your love's grown strong enough to make you bear being laughed at, I'll give you leave to trouble me with it. Till when pray forbear, sir" (4.1).

In the final test of his love Harriet does force Dorimant to be laughed at and to bear it. The rake-hell who had been deeply embarrassed by the scorn of Mrs. Loveit and Bellinda and who had sought revenge on the one and had triumphed over the other's virtue is, in the last few moments of the play, made to confess publicly that he will follow Harriet even to the dull ends of the earth, to her home in Hampshire, where she and her mother and an old lame aunt sit, "moping like three or four melancholy birds in a spacious volary—." Medley, at least, must have snickered at the prospect of his city-bred friend confined to country boredom.

Earlier in *The Man of Mode,* however, Dorimant had had a brief trial run at a staider mode of living and had survived it. When in act 4 Harriet asks him to disguise himself as Mr. Courtage, a "foppish admirer of quality, who . . . never offers love to a woman below a lady-grandmother," Dorimant acts the part with a consummate skill that demonstrates how thoroughly he has mastered the forms of conduct of his society. So successful is he in convincing Lady Woodvill that he is a man of an older mode that she wishes Harriet were free to marry him, and while the episode is a delicious joke on Lady Woodvill, there is also more than a hint here that Harriet has prepared a test for Dorimant and that he has passed it. He has proven that he can fit harmoniously into a much more sedate environment than that to which he is accustomed, perhaps even into life in the country.

According to the most optimistic estimate of their success, Harriet and Dorimant ought to be expected to have a successful marriage. They have discovered throughout the course of the comedy that they have a great deal in common. Both love heroic poetry, the work of Waller in particular, and they even quote lines spontaneously to each other. And, as Kenneth Muir observes, Harriet even reads and quotes from Abraham Cowley's *Davideis,* something we cannot imagine Bellinda or Mrs. Loveit doing.[9] Both Harriet and Dorimant are characterized, as Professor John Barnard has pointed out, by a wildness, a resistance to control by others[10] that promises interesting times in their future relationship. Most important of all, for these two well-to-do members of the idle upper class, is the fact that they are intellectual and conversational equals. Beyond the modest demands upon their time of ombre, tennis, dancing, and the management of their estates, they will be able, we presume, to enjoy perpetually the pleasures of wit-combats like those at their first meeting in the Mall or their exchange at Lady Townley's house (5.2) when Dorimant finds Harriet listening to a song of his own composing:

DORIMANT. What have we here, the picture of celebrated Beauty, giving audience in public to a declared lover?

HARRIET. Play the dying fop, and make the piece complete sir.

DORIMANT. What think you if the hint were well improved? The whole mystery of making love pleasantly designed and wrought in a suit of hangings?

HARRIET. 'Twere needless to execute fools in effigy who suffer daily in their own persons.

Within this witty satire on précieux lovemaking is a clear statement by both lovers that beyond these artificial forms there must be a depth of knowledge of each other that can sustain the love-at-first-sight that has brought them together. They cannot know yet what the audience has seen—their several honest confessions of love. Dorimant has said, "I love her, and dare not let her know it . . ." (4.1), and Harriet has just admitted, "My love springs with my blood into my face, I dare not look upon him yet" (5.2). According to this romantic reading of the courtship of the aging roué and the country maiden, they will soon dare to confess their love and marriage will follow.

"The Great Creature"

The conclusion of the love-combat in *The Man of Mode* is not quite all there is to the final effect of the play, for Sir Fopling Flutter's presence on stage then and his prominent place in the epilogue keep the audience's attention riveted on that man of mode even after the curtain falls. He is the source of much of the heartiest laughter in the comedy, and Dryden's epilogue sums up the hits that have been made along the way—at his singing, talking, posing, his refinement, his perpetual gaiety, his French airs, and, of course, his fashion in clothing. It is very likely that Harriet herself, with her marvelous gift of mimickry, recited the epilogue and acted out many of the lines.

For some readers this emphasis at the end upon a character who is in no way central to the action seems a curious decision on Etherege's part, and the title and subtitle of the play only add to the mystery. Others, for various reasons, have seen Sir Fopling instead as a figure of much comic interest, a truly important part of the movement of the main plot—and as the first and most fully developed of a long succession of stage fops. One of the pioneer critics of Restoration comedy, Vivian de Sola Pinto, has even concluded that Sir Fopling is the high point of the comedy: "The duel between [Harriet] and Dorimant is completely outshone by the blazing of Sir Fopling's folly, which is magnificent . . ."[11]; and in a recent article Wandalie Henshaw even finds Fopling to be "the disconcerting yet reassuring mirror of Etherege's entire world."[12]

The success of Fopling in drawing the audience's attention to himself depends in large measure upon the interpretation of his final appearance by the play's director. If the "great creature," as Gosse called him, is given the full stage across which to make his final entrance—adjusting an enormous periwig and pursued by his page—and upon which to conduct his final flirtation with Mrs. Loveit with its attendant repulse, he cannot help but demand the attention of the audience. Once again, Etherege's eye for laughter-provoking farce is clearly evident. While he is often praised for the wit on display in *The Man of Mode,* Etherege is equally a master of visual comedy, and a skilled director will make the most of the opportunities that Sir Fopling provides.

The 1971 production of *The Man of Mode,* by the Royal Shakespeare Company, appears to have realized many of the opportunities in the play for eliciting laughter by means of visual effects. One scene in particular, directed by Terry Hands and reported to Robert Waterhouse by designer Timothy O'Brien, gives a clear vision of the possibilities in the character of Sir Fopling for lively stage action. O'Brien describes the treatment of act 4, scene 2, shortly after Fopling's arrival at Dorimant's lodging with Medley and Bellair:

Someone says, "Look, Sir Fopling's dancing" and he's up on a cloud at the end of a wonderfully successful party where he has felt himself the real comet in the sky, and he's celebrating this so nakedly in his Brandenberg with its soft colours and weaving about the stage like some marvelously happy moth. Then he explains that he has written a song, which is teased out of him. It's read over and he's persuaded to sing it. He stands on the bed, starts to sing, and suddenly realises it's a much better song than he remembered. Almost with tears of pride he sings. Then he sits down and his friends say: "Of its kind it couldn't be bettered and it's particularly remarkable for being in the French manner." "That's what I aimed at," he says, bursts into tears, and then makes a marvelous gesture: he cries "Slap, down goes the glass and we're at it."[13]

O'Brien goes on to point out that in this scene Sir Fopling Flutter rises above the artificiality that is his trademark, is so enthusiastic and so caught up in the pleasure of his successes that the artificiality disappears. Above all, it is a great scene of visual comedy, at which the audience must laugh in delight as well as in ridicule, and it suggests the potential for farcical treatment in every scene in which Fopling appears.

Sir Fopling Flutter's greater role, however, is as an object of derision for his immoderately effeminate and frenchified manners. The point at which a gentleman's manners become excessively French or excessively extreme in some other way in terms of clothing style, gait, conversation, and so on was a matter of concern to the court-related audience at *The Man of Mode.* French culture had had a powerful influence on all aspects of English social life since well before the Restoration, and conversational expression, as C. D. Cecil has pointed out, was substantially influenced by European standards of elegance, particularly those of the classics and of the French.[14] Thus it is not that

Sir Fopling is a Francophile but that he is an uncritical one. One need only compare him with Dorimant, who has also lived in France, who knows French well, and whose dress—at least while in Paris—was so thoroughly French that in the Tuileries Gardens he was once mistaken for a French gentleman. On the other hand, Dorimant exhibits in London a distinctly English blend of styles in dress and conduct, reflecting judicious selection in order to avoid extremes. Furthermore, the fact that Sir Fopling Flutter is the only character in the comedy who is spoken of as frequenting the court has suggested to one scholar that the educated part of the audience would have understood him to be a criticism of "the French affectations actually to be found there."[15]

In Dorimant and Fopling Etherege might be thought of as putting into dramatic form the definition of true and false wits given by Thomas Hobbes in *Leviathan* (1651): "When a person's words and actions are considered as his owne, then he is called a *Naturall Person*: And when they are considered as representing the words and actions of an other then is he a *Feigned* or *Artificiall person*."[16] Both Dorimant and Sir Fopling Flutter are wits and both are men of mode, the one the true or "natural," the other the false or "artificial."

Etherege, however, has treated his artificial wit lovingly, sympathetically, as a character who is innocent of guile, free of designs upon other people or their property, and almost pathetically unaware that he is a figure of ridicule to the true wits in the play. Lady Townley's brief lecture on politeness in social intercourse helps the audience know how to respond to Sir Fopling: "'Tis good to have an universal taste," she tells Emilia, "we should love wit, but for variety, be able to divert ourselves with the extravagances of those who want it" (3.2). The most sympathetic portrait of the Sir Foplings of the world is that given by Mrs. Loveit to Dorimant (5.1) in defense of her flirtation with Fopling the evening before, and although her praise must be discounted as reflective of her resentment toward Dorimant, the arguments she offers convince us that such "noisy fools" have virtues and a place in the social fabric. First, she says, they truly admire women and do not flatter in order to make conquests; then, their conversation provides pleasant diversion; and finally, they are not guilty of "subtle and causeless jealousies" of the sort that is plaguing Dorimant at that very moment. Mrs. Loveit is almost convincing, but her defense—while it might apply to women of, say, Lady Towley's character—can never suit someone of Loveit's proud and passionate nature. As her name announces, she loves what the harmless fools like Sir Fopling can never deliver, for Sir Fopling himself confides to Medley, after Loveit's fierce rejection of him at the end of act 5, "An intrigue now would be but a temptation to me to throw away that vigour on one which I mean shall shortly make my court to the whole sex in a ballet."

Sir Fopling Flutter differs greatly from the fools in George Etherege's two earlier comedies. He is not a countrified clown like Sir Nicholas Cully or Sir Oliver Cockwood but a widely traveled and refined man of mode whose dress and manners are disturbingly like those in vogue at court. If intelligence be defined as the ability to make fine distinctions, his intelligence is too narrowly focused. The result, however, is not in any way destructive to society. As Susan Staves has pointed out in an article entitled "A Few Kind Words for the Fop,"[17] the qualities that characterize Sir Fopling would be desirable in men today—avoidance of violence, sexual passivity, interest in fashion, and delicacy in matters of cleanliness and odor—except that modern men still scorn the fools who exhibit these in excess. Dorimant pronounces a typical universal and timeless judgment on the matter of male dress and grooming in his exchange with Handy (1.1):

HANDY. Will you use the essence or orange-flower water?

DORIMANT. I will smell as I do today, no offence to the ladies' noses. . . . That a man's excellency should lie in neatly tying of a ribbond, or a cravat! how careful's nature in furnishing the world with necessary coxcombs!

Because *The Man of Mode* has only the slightest of plots, consisting essentially of a series of episodes in which Etherege's principal concern is to move his main character through a succession of love affairs toward something approximating true love, Sir Fopling Flutter's role in that plot is indeed a minor one. Yet he does contribute something to the action, as Derek Hughes has observed,[18] even if it is only to interrupt and thus postpone important developments in Dorimant's halting progression toward happiness. The earliest of these is Dorimant's first meeting with Harriet in the Mall in act 3, scene 3. The flirtation between the two will-be lovers has begun, and then is checked by the arrival of Lady Woodvill. But just as Lady Woodvill is about to discover Dorimant's real identity, Sir Fopling Flutter makes another of his brilliantly farcical entrances, arranging his seven attendants on the stage, calling out Dorimant's name, and thus scattering Lady Woodvill, Harriet, and their small entourage of Busy and Young Bellair. The interruption leaves Dorimant frustrated but unrecognized and leaves the audience, of course, eager for the next stage in this unfolding action.

The next interference by Sir Fopling in Dorimant's progress toward true love comes in act 4, scene 1, and once again it interrupts the conversation of Dorimant and Harriet at a point where their courting has virtually come to a standstill. Harriet has told Dorimant to "forbear" until his love is "strong enough to make [him] bear being laughed at," and so Fopling's entrance with his masked dancers is Etherege's device for delaying the development of their affair until the audience can learn more about their personalities and hence about the likelihood that they are well matched. Such knowledge comes in the exchange that follows, particularly with the revelation that Harriet, like Dorimant, is widely read in French and English literature and that her judgment of Sir Fopling matches his. Next, Sir Fopling and company arrive at Dorimant's rooms just as his lovemaking with Bellinda has ended, thus helping to propel the action in a new direction.

Finally, Sir Fopling contributes in an important way to the resolution of the comedy. As Professor Barnard has correctly pointed out, as long as the focus of attention in the last act is principally upon Dorimant, upon his ruthless treatment of Mrs. Loveit, and upon his apparent fickleness in proposing to continue affairs with her and with Bellinda while engaging himself to Harriet, the possibility of a conventional comic ending is unlikely.[19] Sir Fopling's entrance near the end of act 5 and his rejection by the outraged Loveit, however, keep his foolishness as a center of attention and lead to Harriet's comic speech about the miseries of country life and to the elaborate dance that ends the play. Thus the audience is united in laughter in these last minutes and the dishonesty of Dorimant's earlier actions is forgotten. When Harriet, as we may assume, returns downstage to speak Dryden's epilogue about Sir Fopling Flutter and his fellow fops in the audience, the attention of the amused auditors is drawn even further away from the issue of ethical behavior that has left so many readers uncomfortable.

Chapter Five

Minor Works

Poetry

In addition to constructing popular and influential comedies, throughout his lifetime George Etherege composed poetry, writing out dozens of love songs, satires, and miscellaneous verses that circulated in manuscript and were copied and passed from hand to hand for years until lost or escaped into print. How many pieces he wrote will never be known, and it is certain that we do not have all of them today. In his excellent little collection of Etherege's poetry James Thorpe prints thirty-one poems that can be assigned with assurance to Etherege. He includes six more of doubtful authorship, but leaves out altogether seven brief tavern songs sung by Palmer in *The Comical Revenge,* several songs by Sir Joslin in *She Would If She Could,* as well as a number of poems wrongly attributed to Etherege. Other verses by Etherege, both in manuscript and in print, existed at one time but now are lost. Professor Wilson argues, for example, that the lost lampoons by Etherege and his friends "must have been as numerous as those which survived," and offers as evidence the "numberless ballads" that Count Grammont said were written by that group of wits against Lord Chesterfield and his amorous wife.[1] In one of his manuscript notes, moreover, William Oldys commented that he had once seen a miscellany from 1672 "almost full" of poems by Etherege but without his name attached;[2] and Professor Thorpe, illustrating the ease with which ephemera of this sort disappeared, cites publisher Jacob Tonson: "I have known several Celebrated Pieces so utterly lost in three or four years time after they were written, as not to be recoverable by all the search I cou'd make after 'em."[3] What was impossible for Tonson is certainly so for scholars today, and there is little likelihood of many more additions to the Etherege poetic canon.

Slender as it is, the body of extant verses by George Etherege reinforces his reputation as a witty playwright and genteel companion, as "Gentle George" and "Easy Etherege." While his verses today have few readers and little scholarly attention, in his own time and for decades after his death, his poems were widely known, frequently copied into private collections, set to music by such composers as Henry Purcell, John Eccles, and John Blow, and anthologized in such seventeenth-century miscellanies as *The New Academy of Complements* (1669), *A Collection of Poems, Written upon Several Occasions* (1672), and *Choice Ayres and Songs* (1683). Professor Thorpe reports that he has discovered poems and songs by George Etherege "in more than fifty contemporary manuscripts and in about a hundred and fifty printed books of the Restoration and early eighteenth century," and verses continued to appear from time to time in anthologies in the nineteenth and twentieth centuries, "though frequently without attribution and usually in corrupt form."[4]

The first collection of Etherege's poems under his own name was a slender one, printed by Jacob Tonson in 1704 as the last few pages of the first complete edition of the plays, *The Works of Sir George Etherege: Containing His Plays and Poems*. Tonson found only five poems to add to the fifteen songs already in the comedies, but, taken together, the twenty pieces represent quite well the range of poetic genres that Etherege attempted: dramatic songs, love lyrics, poems of praise, satires, and bawdy verse letters.

Although many of the songs in the plays came to have independent lives of their own by being included in dozens of anthologies in the centuries since they first were sung, their original purpose was to contribute in some way to the action or the characterization. That is the thesis of Professor Boyette's essay on the topic, as a matter of fact, that the songs help to characterize, to "reveal an emotional attitude," "to distinguish a theme, or satirize a traditional ideology, motif, or character."[5] Typical of the songs that reveal character and contribute to mood is one sung by Aurelia and Letitia in act 2, scene 2, of *The Comical Revenge*. When Aurelia, who is suffering from unrequited love for the noble Bruce, discovers that her woman Letitia has also felt love's smart, the two express their hopeless passion in a pastoral of the conventional type:

When Phillis watched her harmless sheep
Not one poor lamb was made a prey;
Yet she had cause enough to weep,
Her silly heart did go astray:

. . .

Then sitting with her arms across,
Her sorrows streaming from each eye;

She fixed her thoughts upon her loss,
And in despair resolved to die.

Etherege's principal purposes in thus underscoring Aurelia's helpless suffering are to make Bruce's falling in love with her more believable, because it is sparked by her passion for him, and to intensify the emotional release felt by the audience when these two star-crossed lovers finally do find each other. There is little to remark about most of these songs, little that is original in metaphor and meaning, for Etherege intended them to be immediately understandable so as to advance the action of the play or contribute to the mood. Nevertheless, as Professor Boyette has discovered, Etherege's songs were more popular as discrete pieces than those by any other major comic dramatist except the great Dryden. Even Sir Fopling's song in *The Man of Mode* (4.2), intended by Etherege as a parody of the conventional lover's complaint, took on new and independent life when freed of the confines of the comedy and was anthologized in a number of popular publications in the early eighteenth century.

The next largest group of poems by Etherege are the love lyrics, often called songs in the anthologies but on the whole distinguishable from the songs in the plays by their greater complexity of figures of speech and images. Professor Thorpe prints twelve of them in his edition (if we exclude two songs intended for plays by Thomas Southerne and Nahum Tate), ranging from the simple "To a Very Young Lady" to the complex, metaphysical "The Divided Heart." The most interesting of these, certainly, is Etherege's most popular poem, "Silvia." It was set to music by four different composers and printed in more than forty anthologies in the seventeenth and eighteenth centuries. A part of its interest lies in Silvia's similarity in appearance and character to the strong-willed Harriet in *The Man of Mode*. Like Harriet, she is "fair and unkind," is witty, beautiful, and independent-minded. The third and final stanza concludes:

The desperate lover can hope no redress
Where beauty and rigor are both in excess;
In Silvia they meet, so unhappy am I,
Who sees her must love and who loves her must die.

Surely in few love lyrics is the word *rigor* applied to the maiden, but Etherege's use of it indicates a more serious theme underlying most of the love lyrics: the virgin who would survive the soft blandishments of the shepherds and wits in Etherege's songs must learn disdain or be undone.

Of Etherege's poems of praise, only two remain—an ecomium to a possible patron and one to a literary acquaintance whose identity is not known. The hoped-for patron was the marchioness of Newcastle, or perhaps her husband, later the duke of Newcastle; and the forty-line poem is full of such hyperbolic expressions as "matchless," "brightest beauty," "charming soul," "victorious eyes," "deathless fame," and "glorious dame." What advantage Etherege might have expected or gotten from this piece of fulsome flattery is not known, but the duke thought highly of the effort and printed it first among the poems honoring his wife in 1676.[6] The second commendatory poem, "To Mr. J. N. on his Translations out of French and Italian," is especially notable because it supports the idea that Etherege knew Italian as well as French. His own lyric, "Garde le secret de ton Ame," written in 1686/87, is evidence of his mastery of conventional French verse, but there is no other certain evidence that he knew Italian. The problem of all translators is captured well in a couplet: "In these attempts so few have had success, / Their beauties suffer in our English dress."

Although we may speculate that Etherege wrote many more satires than have been recovered and attributed to him, the four in Thorpe's edition are probably fair representatives of his "soft Lampoons."[7] The breadth of subject matter among the four is wide, ranging from a laughing look at the lover who—having gained his Phillis's consent—is unable to perform, to an attack on the uxorious earl of Mulgrave, to a satire on ladies who love gambling more than plays and witty men, and to the prologue to Dryden's *Sir Martin Mar-all* in which the taste of the audience and the cupidity of the managers are ridiculed. While each has its own interest—whether verse form, subject matter, figures of speech, or the like—it is the relation of each to Etherege's own career in London that gives them particular value. His reputation as satyr, witty companion, gambler, and man of the theater is reinforced by these productions.

The last major grouping of poems by Etherege consists of a form that he seems to have originated himself, the "ramble," or the verse letter in which the exhausted debauchee reviews his state and considers his options for more indulgence. Professor Earl Miner, in his study of later seventeenth-century poetry, outlines the usual content of such poems: the speaker describes himself as "waking up after debauchery, either once more aroused or, more usually, surfeited and sick, and then going out on the town to agitate the 'sense' again."[8] The earlier of the two extant pairs of "rambles" is directed to Lord Buckhurst, whose friendship probably antedated *The Comical Revenge* (1664) by at least several months. The scabrous details of their sexual escapades and the consequences, expressed in iambic tetrameter couplets, merit no review here. Together with the similar verses written from Ratisbon to Lord Middleton nearly a quarter of a century later, they are full of sexual braggadocio and masculine laughter at the London whores and coarse German women who satisfy Etherege's needs. If there is any unifying ingredient between these rambles and the love songs and love lyrics discussed above, it is in the awareness in both sorts of poetry that the warfare between the sexes is a cruel one. The losers are the heartbroken swains of the love poems and the exploited women of the verse letters—but even the winners must be unhappy, both the cruel-hearted ladies who are all rejection and the poxed and poxing rakes whose excesses must appear grotesque to the sensible reader. Like the world of the plays, the world of most of Etherege's poems is an unpleasant place; unlike the dramatic world there is little of the laughter of comedy to relieve it.

Letters

In his own time Etherege's reputation as a letter writer rested entirely upon the handful of bawdy "rambles" that he exchanged with Lord Buckhurst and perhaps with others. Today, however, thanks to two editions of his correspondence, he is known as the author of more than four hundred letters, a far greater number than can be claimed for any other Restoration dramatist.[9] Almost all of his extensive correspondence, however, consists of official dispatches that he mailed back to London from his post at Ratisbon, Germany. As King James II's resident for three years at the capital of the Holy Roman Empire (late 1685 to early 1689), he was responsible for representing his nation in ceremonial affairs and—more significant—supplying Secretary of State Middleton with important political and military news as it could be gathered from throughout central Europe. Although Sir George and his secretary were especially assiduous in keeping copies of the offical dispatches, a number of Etherege's personal letters were also preserved. Of the more than four hundred letters extant, perhaps fifteen percent are familiar letters to friends, and they are complemented by witty remarks and trenchant observations scattered throughout nearly all of the correspondence.

The portrait that emerges out of the hundreds of pages of printed and manuscript letters is of Sir George as very much a man of business in addition to his image as a man of wit and leisure. He was punctual to a fault in reporting to Lord Middleton with every post, sending his twice-weekly dispatches almost without fail throughout his three-year term and requesting again and again that any faults or oversights be called to his attention so that he could correct them promptly. His loyalty to King James is beyond question, and from early 1688 and on, as the threat from William of Orange became more and more apparent, Etherege's voice grows increasingly shrill as he denounces Protestant ambitions and supports the king and his party.

On 13 December 1685, shortly after his arrival in Ratisbon, he wrote to Lord Middleton, explaining his method for reporting: "I expect howerly the news from Vienna. if it comes in time I will enclose it. The Post comes from that place unluckely ye very two days our post serves for London and I fear now the winter begins to be more severe it will come so late I shall not be able to send you the news so fresh as I wou'd do." If he is sending too much news, Etherege observes, he will try to be more concise. "Correct my faults," he pleads, "and they shalbe mended."[10] The same letter includes a passage that can serve to exemplify the brevity in reporting for which Etherege strove:

> I rec'd just now a note wch tells me it is confidently writ from Berlin that the Counte de Rebenac, Envoyeé from ffrance, had ask'd of the Elector an assurance in writing by wch he shou'd promise to the King his Maister not to break the Treaty he had made with him, much less to make any new Alliances or renew the old, without his aprobation, wch the Elector refus'd to do, on wch the Envoyeé seem'd much discontented and was about taking his leave wch gave the Court an oportunity in their turn to show they were not much concern'd at it.

There is a good deal more of the same sort of accurate, insightful, and concise interpretation in the letter; and indeed the great body of Etherege's correspondence, including more than eighty complete letters still in manuscript, consists of essentially this kind of detailed political reporting. As Etherege wrote to Middleton a few months later, apologizing again for including so much boring minutiae, "but forgive me the pattern I have sent you, and I will trouble you with no more of the stuff."[11] The further value of these detailed reports over the three-year period must be to the historian who wishes to see the European political and military events of 1686–1688 through a pair of keen English eyes.

A copy of each official letter sent back to England was recorded by Etherege's secretary Hugo Hughes in a letterbook, much as secretaries today keep carbon copies, photocopies, or computer entries. Hughes also kept a second letterbook, a secret one in which he copied out some of Etherege's personal letters and kept track of any information that might reflect unfavorably on his master. Hughes's insidious care paid off, for in the spring of 1689, following Sir George's flight to Paris, Hughes was named by William III as Resident to the Diet at Ratisbon at a salary of three hundred pounds per year.[12]

Hugo Hughes also kept a calendar of some of the letters that were not copied into either letterbook. For the most part these were too personal or too petty to be written out in full, although many of them were briefly summarized in a sentence or two. For students of Etherege's plays the entries are especially tantalizing, for many of the letters listed are to Etherege's best friends in England and to his wife and other members of the family. What did Etherege say to Robert Corbet, for example, a gambler friend, to whom he wrote seven letters that are not extant; what did Etherege write in four letters to his friend Tom Maule, or in ten to his nephew George Etherege, or in four to his brother Richard? There are no extant letters to his mother Mary Newstead, yet Etherege wrote to her at least three times; and there is only one letter to his wife, Lady Mary, of twenty-two that are recorded in the catalogue in Hughes's letterbooks. Perhaps most intriguing to us are the two or three missing letters that are known to have been sent to John Dryden.[13] The one letter to Dryden that is extant and that was copied out by Hughes in both letterbooks (20 March 1687) exhibits the best virtues of Etherege's epistolary style, as this opening passage indicates:

> You know I am noe Flatterer, and therefore will excuse me when I tell you I cannot endure you should arrogate a thing to your self you have not the least pretence to. Is it not enough that you excell in soe many eminent vertues, but you must be putting in for a vice which all the world knows is properly my Province. If you persist in your claim to Laziness, you will be

> thought as affected in it as Montaigne is, when he complaines of want of memory. What soul has ever been more active than your own? What Country, nay what corner of the earth, has it not travell'd into? Whose bosom has it not div'd into, and inform'd itself there soe perfectly of all the Secrets of man's heart that onely the great being (whose Image it bears) knows them better? I (whose every action of my life is a witness of my Idlenesse) little thought that you, who have rais'd so many Immortall monuments of your Industrie, durst have set up to be my Rival; but to punish you, I will distinguish. You have noe share in that noble Lazinesse of the minde, which all I write make out my just title to. But as for that of the body, I can let you come in for a Snack without any Jealousy.

Here is that clarity of expression, variety in sentence patterns, and emphatic arrangement that characterize the new English prose of the late seventeenth century. Etherege might have been an influential essayist had he lived in the time of the *Tatler* and the *Spectator*. Dryden's praise for his style, even allowing for a bit of gentlemanly exaggeration, is sincere and very nearly accurate: "I will never enter the lists in Prose with the undoubted best author of it which our nation has produced."[14]

Beyond the witty personal letters, to Dryden, Middleton, the earl of Sunderland, Lord Buckhurst (now the earl of Dorset), and others among his old London friends, Etherege managed to enliven much of the rest of his correspondence with entertaining anecdotes, old and new gossip, insights into the way of life of a London rake in staid Ratisbon, some brilliant character sketches, and of course an *embarras* of clever expressions. By the summer of 1688, however, Etherege is composing his last warm and witty personal letters to friends in London. On 26 August he can still write to William Jephson that he is dozing away his time in Ratisbon, and a few days later to Robert Corbet that he is whiling away the hours in sighing and languishing for the unresponsive Ratisbon women. But soon after, the tone of the correspondence grows profoundly serious. The rumors out of Holland are beginning to be confirmed. To the earl of Carlingford he writes, "So great an armement was never made by sea and Land in Holland since they were a state" (22 September 1688). Within a few more days Etherege warns that the Prince of Orange is now at sea, and yet there is no news from England that defensive preparations are under way. Soon every letter is given over to news and rumors about William's intentions and about the stances being taken by various European states. Soon, too, the tone of concern begins to intensify; the letters become strident outbursts of anger against William and his supporters and passionate expressions of loyalty to King James. Like his father before him—and perhaps *because* of the example of his father—Etherege never wavered in his support for his sovereign. When the end finally came for Etherege's hopes—as it did with the news of King James's arrival in Paris—Etherege quickly left to join him, taking along his copy of the letterbook that was the official record of his loyal service to the last Catholic king in the history of England.

Chapter Six
Epilogue

The life and works of Sir George Etherege have become a fertile field for study and research in the twentieth century, and this after two hundred years in which little was known about him and little interest was envinced in what he had written. The playwright who was praised as England's prose master by John Dryden and two of whose comedies were remarkable popular successes, fell into disfavor in the later eighteenth century. His plays disappeared from the stage entirely thereafter. The discoveries of Dorothy Foster and Frederick Bracher in the recent past, however, have made it possible to see Etherege and his works in a new light, and the present study relies as much as possible on that illumination. There have even been successful stage revivals of two of the comedies in the 1970s and 1980s, and these have been noted in the appropriate places. Although Etherege has hardly been elevated to the first rank of English dramatists by this new interest, he has at least maintained his position as one of the five great comedians of the Restoration period, historically linked with Wycherley, Congreve, Vanbrugh, and Farquhar; and he has become the best-known of all of them and indeed of all of his literary contemporaries through his extensive correspondence, now published and widely known.

The present study relies extensively on the lawsuit material discovered by Professor Foster in reconstructing the environment in which young George Etherege grew up and in filling in details about the family and friends who made up the most influential part of that environment. Etherege seems to have had several of them in mind as he wrote his three plays, particularly *The Comical Revenge,* for the situations on stage and even some of the personages look to us like variations on the real world and the real people who emerge from the pages of testimony taken at the Bull Inn in Maidenhead in 1656 and 1657. Etherege's widowed mother appears, in somewhat altered form, in *The Comical Revenge,* and his sisters may have served as models for the Jolly heiresses in *She Would If She Could.* The most interesting of the many likely identifications are of Grandfather Etherege as Lord

Bevill and Captain George Etherege as Bruce in *The Comical Revenge*. There the playwright created a strong-willed family head (like Grandfather Etherege, a widower) and a noble young Royalist who—like Etherege's father—has devoted himself entirely to his sovereign and now must suffer for it.

The facts of George Etherege's early life strongly reinforce many of the themes in the comedies and help to explain his loyalty to King James in the 1680s. Because of the Civil War, Etherege's father lost his livelihood and shortly after went into exile in France, there to die in 1650 without seeing his family again. His position as a purveyor to the Catholic Queen Henrietta Maria was unpopular with his family's Puritan neighbors, and Mary Etherege's second marriage in 1652 to a suspected Royalist could only have continued that antipathy. Moreover, the small estate that was intended for young George by his grandfather was for a long time jeopardized by Uncle John Etherege, a divine and an enemy to the Royalist cause and to George's father, whom John considered a rebel. It is not surprising, then, that in the comedies the preachers and Puritans are treated as villains or fools and that in the letters, particularly in late 1688, Etherege's loyalty to Catholic King James appears almost obsessive.

Between 1654 and 1659 Etherege served as an apprentice to Beaconsfield attorney George Gosnold, and he later studied law for a time at Clement's Inn, in the parish of his father's birth. It was almost certainly during this time in London that he became familiar with stage plays, and when he came to write his own three comedies, he relied heavily upon his knowledge of the law in the creation of characters and situations. Some idea of his knowledge of jurisprudence can be seen, nearly thirty years after he left Gosnold, in the letters he wrote from Ratisbon, for many of them are thoroughgoing analyses of issues in English law.

The success on stage of George Etherege's plays depended as much upon performance as upon script, and the outstanding success of *The Comical Revenge* resulted from the two in perfect combination. Produced at the Duke's Playhouse by Davenant's popular company, *The Comical Revenge* enjoyed the longest recorded run of any London play since the Restoration and brought Etherege a substantial income. While the play itself was an ingenious composite of a number of popular ingredients—heroic lovers, a "gay" couple, confidence schemes, and plenty of farce—it was the character of Sir Frederick Frollick that gave the play its fresh appeal. As a representative of the "extravagant rake," Sir Frederick might have been modeled after one of the wild young lords of Etherege's acquaintance whose scandalous escapades were legendary. More important than his lively libertinism is the fact that Sir Frederick Frollick proves to be a controlling force in both the upper and the lower plots, and in his solving of a variety of society's problems demonstrates that he has the judgment to form a happy alliance with the Widow Rich.

In striking contrast to the success of *The Comical Revenge* was the signal failure of *She Would If She Could* four years later. Although the occasion was an auspicious one, with the Duke's House crowded to capacity with courtiers and citizens, the audience was not pleased, and Etherege afterward did "mightily find fault" with the production, especially with the poor acting and singing. Had it succeeded as it ought, *She Would If She Could* might well have been followed by many comedies that featured pairs of liberated young women as heroines. As it is, Gatty and Ariana are unique creations, very nearly as dominant in *She Would If She Could* as Sir Frederick is in *The Comical Revenge*. It is their degree of financial independence that helps to make them unusual, coupled with their honest and realistic awareness that it is possible to play the game of life and love by the rules and even—with a little luck—to win. If there is to be happiness in marriage, Etherege is saying in this play, there must be a high degree of freedom on both sides. Where that freedom is lacking, as it is in the Cockwood marriage, misery is the likely result.

A far more profound treatment of the question of happiness in marriage lies at the heart of *The Man of Mode, or, Sir Fopling Flutter,* Etherege's final play. Because of the special care taken by Etherege and the playhouse managers, *The Man of Mode* was a triumphant success at its opening and enjoyed many revivals well into the next century. Its influence on the comedy of the time was minimal, however, primarily because in the two principals, Dorimant and Harriet, Etherege created characters almost too complex and troublesome for comic treatment. With Sir Fopling Flutter, of course, he invented the archetype for a whole series of stage fops, climaxed, many would say, by Lord Foppington in John Vanbrugh's *The Relapse*. *The Man of Mode* has continued to be controversial right up to the present, having as many interpretations as there are critics.

Etherege's Reputation

Over the three centuries since George Etherege wrote, his reputation has rested principally, but not exclusively, upon *The Man of*

Mode. It was frequently said in the decades after his death that in his plays Restoration society was first able to see itself portrayed on stage in its own manner and conversation. Rochester early recognized his friend's genius for conversation and described him as having written "two Talking Plays without one Plot."[1] In his *Account of the English Dramatick Poets* (1691) Gerard Langbaine praised the characters in *The Man of Mode* as "drawn to the Life," and Charles Gildon (1699) reported on the extraordinary success of *The Man of Mode,* also emphasizing the play's realism: "all agreeing it to be true Comedy, and the Characters drawn to the Life."[2] Gildon also linked Etherege to Wycherley and Vanbrugh, thus beginning the practice of identifying these three in the top group of "modern writers of comedy." In 1702 John Dennis praised the realism of the characters in *She Would If She Could* as well as the "freshness and easie grace of its Dialogue."

Within a few years, however, the critical attitude toward Etherege began to change. Richard Steele attacked *The Man of Mode* in the *Spectator* (15 May and 26 May 1711) as "a perfect Contradiction to good Manners, good Sense, and common Honesty" and a picture of "Nature in its utmost Corruption and Degeneracy." Despite occasional objections (notably by Dennis in 1722) to this insistence that comedy ought to portray exemplary rather than reprehensible characters, Steele's was a perspective that prevailed right up until the twentieth century. In his reference guide David Mann presents a litany of eighteenth- and nineteenth-century complaints about the immorality of Etherege's plays that explains why they were not performed and had—until Edmund Gosse's influential article (1881)[3]—only antiquarian interest. Particularly influential was Thomas Babington Macaulay's disapproving piece in the *Edinburgh Review* (January 1841). In reviewing Leigh Hunt's edition of the four great comic dramatists of the Restoration—Wycherley, Congreve, Vanbrugh, and Farquhar—Macaulay condemned their work as immoral and added that of Etherege into the bargain. In doing so, he effectively countered the approving comments of William Hazlitt and Charles Lamb of twenty years previous.

With Gosse, the issue of morality is no longer of significance; once again the plays are realistic pictures of upper-class society, and Etherege is an innovative writer of comedy and an effective diplomat. Five reprintings of Gosse's article appeared over the next two decades, evidence of the growing interest in Etherege's work, and a new collected edition by A. W. Verity in 1888, the first in 153 years, made all of the plays readily accessible to new generations of readers.

Despite these late-Victorian efforts, serious study of Etherege's life and work had its greatest stimulus in 1913 with the publication of John Palmer's collection of essays about the five great comic dramatists of the Restoration period. By treating their plays as worthy of serious attention, Palmer helped to inspire in the 1920s an outpouring of books about and editions of genteel comedy that has been rivaled only in the past two decades. "The English comedy of manners," he wrote, "began with Etherege; rose to perfection in Congreve; declined by easy stages with Vanbrugh and Farquhar; and was finally extinguished in Sheridan and Goldsmith."[4] It is a pronouncement that critics have been debating ever since.

As Professor Mann's work shows, in the 1920s and early 1930s full editions of the plays of Congreve, Wycherley, Shadwell, Vanbrugh, Sedley, Farquhar, and Etherege appeared in rapid succession. In the case of Etherege, the least-known of the seventeenth-century dramatists became overnight the best-known because Dorothy Foster published her extensive new information about Etherege's family in eight essays, and Sybil Rosenfeld edited for Oxford University Press the secret letterbook that Hugo Hughes had kept throughout Sir George's three years as English Resident in Ratisbon. Moreover, Etherege was given important consideration in a number of critical studies of Restoration drama that appeared during the decade. Allardyce Nicoll gave high praise to *The Man of Mode* as manners comedy, H. T. E. Perry found Etherege's Dorimant to be a masterly depiction of the fashionable hero of the age, and Kathleen Lynch argued that Etherege's principal contribution to Restoration comedy was a realistic representation of contemporary society. Other critics were less positive in their estimates, some—like Bonamy Dobrée—ambivalent about Etherege's contribution, others continuing to dismiss his comedies as licentious and artificial.

In the 1930s and 1940s Etherege received relatively little attention, although Eleanore Boswell turned up new facts about his life, Sybil Rosenfeld examined his letters in the Middleton Papers, and J. W. Nichol found new information about his wife. Two particularly influential pieces appeared: L. C. Knights's attack on Restoration comedy as "trivial, gross, and dull" and on *The Man of Mode* as shallow; and John Harrington Smith's chapter on Etherege in *The Gay Couple in Restoration Comedy*. Etherege's first two comedies are harmless love-games by "gay couples," said Smith; his last is "cynical comedy" in which love becomes serious.

From the 1950s to the present, however, Etherege's plays have been the object of rapidly growing interest, new facts about his life and career have continued to be uncovered and applied to an understanding of his writing, and new approaches to his works have been undertaken. Once again, David Mann's guide is invaluable as a review of the wide range of criticism. Included are such subjects as Etherege's treatment of wit, of women, of the précieuse tradition, of the rake-heroes and the fops, of marriage, of "type characters" and humors characters, and his use of Molière's plays. The single most influential study of Etherege's comedies has been that by Dale Underwood (1957), an examination of the two ideas that have shaped the protagonists in much of Restoration comedy—the *honnête homme,* from the heroic-romantic tradition, and the libertine, based on Hobbes and Machiavelli. Although little is new in the discussions of Etherege's first two plays, Underwood's analysis of the values in *The Man of Mode* is particularly penetrating. Dorimant is no longer simply a pleasure-loving man-about-town in pursuit of variety in amours but now exhibits "a Hobbesian aggressiveness, competitiveness, and drive for power and 'glory'; a Machiavellian dissembling and cunning [and] an egoistic assertion of self through the control of others."[5] Valuable as it is, and Underwood's study has provoked responses by nearly every critic who has since written about Etherege's comedy, its chief weakness is in its failure to show how this intricate examination of the historical roots of libertinism can be connected directly with George Etherege.

Such connections have yet to be made in most of the criticism that has been written over the subsequent three decades, although, as Professor Mann notes, the long-neglected study of Etherege's library might reveal much about his interests and reading. Professor N. J. Rigaud's "Observations" about that library suggest some of the directions that might be taken. Her conclusions from an examination of the books are that Etherege took his assignment as Resident seriously, that he was concerned about the relation of religion to politics, and that he had a continuing interest in Turkey and its influence on European politics.[6] The most important and influential events in Etherege studies since Underwood's book have been the publication of the poems by Thorpe, the letters by Bracher, and the appearance of a number of articles and chapters that have advanced our knowledge of the playwright's life and accomplishments. Four essays by Frederick Bracher, along with a full introduction to *Letters,* have added greatly to our knowledge of the man, in particular during the period after 1659 when Etherege became a student of law at Clement's Inn. Recent new editions of individual plays are too numerous to discuss, although Michael Cordner's modernized edition of the *Plays* (1982) is important as the first collection since 1927.

Of the many shorter works over the past three decades, those by half a dozen scholars offer especially important new perspectives on Etherege's comedies, namely, the work of David S. Berkeley and C. D. Cecil on the importance of *préciosité* to an understanding of the plays; Ronald Berman's argument that the comic attitudes of *The Man of Mode* are dependent upon the values expressed by Waller in his poetry; Rose Zimbardo's 1981 essay on Harriet in *The Man of Mode* as the "classic comic woman" who serves as an instrument of nature to undermine the heroic pretensions of the protagonist Dorimant; and the recent article by John Barnard (1984) that carefully constructs a picture of the audience for whom Etherege intended *The Man of Mode,* in particular using the evidence of allusions to contemporary operas and to French literature in order to do so. Special notice must also be taken of the work of Robert D. Hume. Basing his judgment on the reading of five hundred seventeenth-century plays, Hume draws four important conclusions: that *She Would If She Could* does not start a new trend in comedy, that *The Man of Mode* should be classified as wit comedy, that it does not reflect daily life, and that Dorimant is a "glamorous but reprehensible" protagonist who "meets his match in a woman cold and tough enough to get him where she wants him."[7] In his recent study, *The Rakish Stage* (1983), Hume draws two additional conclusions that bear directly on the long controversy over the meaning of Etherege's plays, *The Man of Mode* in particular: "There is no instance in late seventeenth-century comedy in which 'libertinism' is presented both seriously and favorably," and "I have never found a play which seemed to me genuinely to attack marriage as an institution or to envisage any serious alternative."[8]

From this brief survey of Etherege studies it is evident that in the twentieth century his works are being taken seriously by scholars for the first time and that the attention being given to him is accelerating. One or another of his comedies is to be found in nearly every new anthology of Restoration plays that appears, and new editions of individual comedies have been proliferating. Allowing for the small number of plays that he wrote, he has in recent years attained a very high stature, unquestionably rivaling the group of four other writers of Restoration comedy with whom he has been linked since Gosse's essay in 1881. Certainly more attention needs to be given to the relationship between Etherege's works and his life and his careers. What is needed more than anything else to give him the wider readership he deserves is a new and inexpensive edition of his works that includes his plays, the complete poems, and a generous selection of those witty and detailed letters that capture so remarkably well the character of the young man who came up to London and there "played the fool in verse and prose" so well that he immortalized himself.

Notes and References

Chapter One

1. Edmund Gosse, "Sir George Etheredge. A Neglected Chapter of English Literature," *Cornhill Magazine,* 43 (1881), 284, 304n, reprinted in *Seventeenth Century Studies* (London, 1883). On page 304n Gosse announces, "It is to the kindness of my friend Mr. Edward Scott that I owe the discovery of The Letterbook." Foster's discoveries are printed in a number of articles under various titles. These are listed in the Selected Bibliography. Strangely enough, until Frederick Bracher's recent work, the lawsuit material has been overlooked or disregarded in nearly every work since published on Etherege.

2. Charles Gildon, additions to Gerard Langbaine's *The Lives and Characters of the English Dramatick Poets* (London, 1698), 53.

3. William Oldys, "Sir George Etherege," *Biographia Britannica* (London, 1750), 3: 1841. A family tree made in 1965 by Geoffrey Martin, a descendant, is in the Houghton Library, Harvard. Frederick Bracher calls attention to its existence in *Letters of Sir George Etherege* (Berkeley: University of California Press, 1974), vii.

4. For the most part, I have relied throughout the pages that deal with Etherege's life to 1660 upon the material uncovered by Miss Foster and printed in the dozen articles to which I have already referred. The discoveries of other scholars are credited individually.

5. Rixman was buried near Maidenhead in the chapel of Bray Church, where Sir George's parents were to be married fourteen years later (J. Wesley Walker, *A History of Maidenhead* [1931; reprint, Maidenhead: Thames Valley Press, 1971], 205).

6. In the record of a Bermuda property transfer in 1643, however, he is still described as "vintner," Foster, *N&Q* (10 December 1927), 417.

7. Pamela Stewart, assistant diocesan archivist, kindly supplied the date of marriage from the transcript of the Bray register now in the Diocesan Record Office, Salisbury. She informs me that Mary Powney's birth year of 1612 is recorded in the Old Windsor transcript, but the month and day are not legible. "It was probably one of the later months of the year," she writes, "as only about two baptisms down, the date '5 Dec.' is shown." In the 1657 lawsuit Mary estimated her age, with becoming modesty, at about 40 years. Miss Stewart was also able to find for me the dates of baptism for several more Powney children—Thomas (2 September 1614), Hannah (29 October 1616), Francis (daughter, 25 January 1617/18), and John (29 September 1619). The Old Windsor transcripts exist only for 1612–1623, 1628, 1631, 1634, and 1635, and there may have been other children born in the missing

years. The name of another son William is to be found in Charles Kerry, *The History and Antiquities of the Hundred of Bray* (London, 1861), opposite 148.

8. In 1927 Miss Foster noted that the Bray parish registers were not extant between 1635 and 1652, and Pamela Stewart reports that there are no transcripts in the Diocesan Record Office between 1635 and 1668. The names of the Etherege children are recorded in the 1656–57 lawsuit and in other material turned up by Miss Foster. The date of Anne's christening is supplied by Miss Stewart; Professor Bracher prints it in *Letters,* xiv.

9. Oldys gives the year as 1636; Dryden makes Etherege a year older in a verse poem of about June 1686 that was forwarded by the Earl of Middleton to Ratisbon:

> To you who live in chill degree,
> (As map informs) of fifty-three,
> And do not much for cold atone
> By bringing thither fifty-one, . . .

James Thorpe (*The Poems of Sir George Etherege* [Princeton: Princeton University Press, 1963], 119–20) argues that Dryden was not an intimate friend and would not have known the year of birth. Etherege himself notes that he was past fifty in May 1688 (*Letters,* 199, 201).

10. It is unlikely that any of the children were born at Whitehall; no record of that fact remains. K. C. Harrison, Westminster City Librarian, has been kind enough to search the parish registers of St. Clement Danes, St. Martin-in-the-Fields, St. Mary-le-Strand, St. Margaret, Westminster, and Westminster Abbey. No Etherege is recorded there.

11. Professor Foster printed the 1657 deposition of Richard Powney in which the details of the purchase are revealed (*N&Q* [17 December 1927], 435); Eleanore Boswell (*Review of English Studies,* 7 [April 1931], 207–9) reexamined the lawsuit materials not long after and discovered that the office was that of purveyor to the queen, although the interrogatory that she quotes names £300 as the purchase price. The full price was £600, with Powney and Grandfather Etherege each paying one half.

12. Leslie Hotson, *The Commonwealth and Restoration Stage* (1928; reprint, New York: Russell & Russell, 1962), 3.

13. Cf. G. E. Aylmer, "The Last Years of Purveyance, 1610–60," *Economic History Review,* 2d Series, 10 (1957–58):84.

14. The question asked was whether Etherege "enjoyed the office during his life?" (Boswell, *Review of English Studies* [1931], 207). Foster discovered the date of Captain Etherege's death in Mary's deposition in 1657, but mistook the year as 1649 (*N&Q* [17 December 1927], 437). She published the correction in *Review of English Studies,* 8 (October 1932), 459.

15. Cited in *Letters,* xv; Foster, *N&Q,* 17 December 1927, 435.

16. *Letters,* 248; hereafter cited in text.

17. D. H. Pennington suggests that the collapse of the London government was very slow and that the legal system in particular remained substantially intact until late in 1643 ("The Rebels of 1642," in *The English Civil War and After, 1642–1658,* ed. R. H. Parry [Berkeley and Los Angeles: University of California Press, 1970], 36–37).

18. "A Deep Sigh Breathed Through the Lodgings at White Hall Deploring the absence of the Court, and the Miseries of the Pallace," cited in Hotson, *Commonwealth,* 10.

19. John Howard Brown and W. Guest, *History of Thame* (Thame, 1935), 112, cited in *Letters,* xv note; Oldys, *Biographia,* 1841.

20. *The Letterbook of Sir George Etherege,* ed. Sybil Rosenfeld (1928; reprint, New York: Benjamin Blom, 1971), 293. The verses "Upon Love," perhaps by Etherege, contain lines that refer to his father and grandfather: "I speak my sire's and grand-sire's praise, / Tell her [his mistress] how brave, how good he was." Captain Etherege could have been described as brave in following his queen to France, and Grandfather Etherege was good—to his grandchildren in particular. Although Thorpe (*Poems,* 130–31) considers the verses not to be in Etherege's manner and lists them among those of doubtful authorship, the references to sire and grandsire, and to money as the "common barrator" that makes children disobey, would have obvious relevance to Etherege. The poem was attributed to him in Buckingham's *Miscellaneous Works* (London, 1705), but attributions in that work are frequently unreliable.

21. Foster, *N&Q* (10 December 1927), 418n.

22. The phrase is used by Francis Hawkins (*Youths Behaviour,* or *Decency in Conversation Amongst Men* [London, 1641/1663], 60) in an addition dated 1656, showing that stylish dress was of interest to the modish well before Charles returned from the Continent.

23. Walker, *A History of Maidenhead,* 95; Kerry, *History . . . of Bray,* 146.

24. Ever since his marriage in 1652 to the widowed Mary, said Newstead, "George Etherege the elder hath bine at the Charge of mainteyning two of the Children . . . , and Master Powney hath mainteyned an other of the Children, and this deponent likewise mainteyned an other of the said Children" (Foster, *N&Q,* 17 December 1927, 438).

25. Walker, *History,* 45.

26. Foster, *N&Q,* 24 December 1927, 454n.

27. Roe was author of the manuscript *A Compendious Relation of the Proceedings and Acts of the Imperial Dyet Held at Ratisbon in 1640 and 1641,* which may have been read by Etherege before he left to become English Resident in Ratisbon in 1685.

28. Anne's will, however, makes provision for mourning rings to be

given "Lady Lockhart and her two Daughters" in Scotland, and Lady Lockhart's picture is bequeathed to John Powney's wife.

29. Exactly when the event occurred cannot be determined from the lawsuit material. Foster believed that the year was 1653 (*N&Q,* 24 December 1927, 454), but the testimony of Mary and Christopher Newstead argues for 1654. In April 1657 Newstead deposed that he had heard that George had been placed about two-and-a-half years earlier (i.e., October 1654); Mary testified that George's placing was "about Three yeares since," or April 1654 (*N&Q,* 17 December 1927, 438–39). Eleanore Boswell discovered from a 1699 lawsuit that Gosnold was at Beaconsfield (*RES,* 208–9). Frederick Bracher notes that Etherege's signature as witness is found on Gosnold's documents beginning in 1656 ("Etherege at Clement's Inn," *Huntington Library Quarterly,* 43 [Spring 1980]: 127).

30. One of the arresting officers was described by Thomas Ellwood as "a brisk, genteel young man, a shopkeeper in the town, whose name was Cherry." This would have been one of Thomas Cherry's sons, perhaps the one who with his father had witnessed Etherege's May indenture (Walker, *History,* 122–23).

31. Boswell, *RES,* 208, has established his death as occurring between 5 March and 30 April. We know from Anne Etherege's will (printed by Foster) that her grandfather was buried in Bray Church, but a new floor now covers the markers there, and so the date of burial is not accessible.

32. Foster, *N&Q,* 17 December 1927, 438.

33. Foster cites Richard Norwood's survey of 1662/63, when the land was in Henry Moore's possession (*N&Q,* 13 May 1922, 364).

34. Gregory King's "Tables" of 1688 show the per capita income for each family in various social classes. Thus Etherege's £40 a year puts him just below the Esquires (averaging £45 per person in the household), and well above Gentlemen (£33 per person), Lesser Merchants (£33), Persons in greater offices (£30), and Persons in the law (£22) (Charles Davenant, *Works* [London, 1771], vol. 2, 184). Etherege's position in 1658 would have been better than it appears because of inflation over the next thirty years. In 1653–1662 the yearly wage of a plumber, interestingly enough, the best paid of the workmen, was £40 (H. D. Traill and J. S. Mann, eds., *Social England,* vol. 4, 1603–1714 [London, Paris, New York, and Melbourne: Cassell & Co., 1903], 376).

35. Bracher, "Etherege at Clement's Inn," 132–33.

36. Walker, *History,* 94.

37. On 27 September 1699, his brother-in-law Samuel Ferrers identified Etherege's signature on a document dated 14 August 1658; and he deposed that on that date Etherege was Gosnold's apprentice (Boswell, *RES,* 208). After that date, however, other men sign as witnesses: presumably Etherege has left Beaconsfield (Frederick Bracher, "Etherege at Clement's Inn," 28).

38. Boswell, *RES,* 208.

39. Bracher, "Etherege at Clement's Inn," 127–34. Bracher's adventures in turning up the fact of Etherege's enrolling at Clement's Inn deserve comment. In the fall of 1976, having discovered an indirect connection between Gosnold and Clement's Inn, Bracher looked about in London for some evidence that Etherege might have gone there for further study. On the last day before his scheduled return to America, Bracher still had discovered nothing. He flipped a mental coin by deciding to go where the next bus took him. It took him to the Public Record Office, where by chance a young lady at an "Inqueries" desk recalled a few private documents left at the PRO for safekeeping. Among them, it turned out, was a volume entitled "Clement's Inn Admissions Book 1655–1790" and on page 6 the long-sought reference. I have consulted a photocopy of the page in obtaining the names of those enrolled at about the same time as Etherege.

40. Rosemary June Beless, "Reflections of the Law in the Comedies of Etherege, Wycherley, and Congreve," Ph.D. dissertation, University of Utah, 1977, 133–34.

41. *A Calendar of the Middle Temple Records,* ed. C. H. Hopwood (London, 1903), xx, 166–67; and *A Calendar of the Inner Temple Records,* ed. F. A. Inderwick (London, 1896), vol. 2, 328. Both are cited by Bracher, "Etherege at Clement's Inn," 131, as are the surreptitious performances noted below.

42. Many years later Etherege seems to have remembered the phrasing of his own similitude in a letter to a friend: "It would be as impertinent in me as if a Sollicitor or an Atturny shou'd entertain a man who hates a Law Suite with all the causes depending in his County" (*Letters,* 168).

43. Foster, *N&Q,* 17 December 1927, 439–40. The W. Glascocke who signed the order may be the same William Glascocke, J. P., who was addressed by Sir William Davenant in a document of 20 August 1660, designed to regulate the theaters (Hotson, *Commonwealth,* 202).

44. A manuscript family tree of the Ethereges, presented to the Houghton Library, Harvard, by Godfrey Martin, says that young George Etherege met Charles II when he was in Paris before 1660. There is no confirming evidence.

45. Thorpe notes that the poem imitates one in French by Charles Beys (1652). That Etherege's poem dates from the period 1660–1662 is suggested by its place among dated poems in the National Library of Scotland (*Poems,* 77–78).

46. Bertha Porter, "Newstead, Christopher," *Dictionary of National Biography,* ed. Sidney Lee and Leslie Stephen (London, 1921–22), vol. 14, 362. The account is almost certainly in error since Porter names only Newstead's wife Mary Fullhurst, whom he married in 1631, and says nothing of a second marriage. See also my article, "The Mother of Sir George Etherege," *N&Q,* 22 (June 1975):262–64.

47. PRO, Reference Prob 11/310.

48. Since Evelyn saw the play on 27 April, it probably premiered before Passion Week, 4–10 April (cf. William Van Lennep, ed., *The London Stage, Part 1: 1660–1700* [Carbondale, Ill.: Southern Illinois University Press, 1965], 76).

49. John Downes, *Roscius Anglicanus* (London, 1708), 25. Downes was bookkeeper and prompter at Lincoln's Inn Fields from 1662 to 1706.

50. John Evelyn, *Diary,* 5 February 1664.

51. Elizabeth Scanlan's study concludes that the following seating capacity would be reasonable at the Duke's House: pit 100, boxes 122, gallery 130 ("Tennis-Court Theatres and the Duke's Playhouse, 1661–1671," Ph.D. dissertation, Columbia University, 1952, 286). Basic charges at both houses were boxes 4 sh., gallery 1 sh. and 1 sh.6d, and pit 2 sh.6d (Emmett L. Avery and Arthur H. Scouten, "Introduction," *London Stage, Part 1,* lxx).

52. A run of 12 or 13 days marked a major stage success by either company. Davenant had opened the new playhouse in June 1661 with his own opera *The Siege of Rhodes* (12 consecutive performances), and in December 1663 an adaptation of *Henry VIII* had run for about 16 nights with no other play intervening (*The London Stage, Part 1,* 72–73).

53. Grandfather George Etherege's home parish, coincidentally, where all his children (including the playwright's father) had been born.

54. Hotson, *Commonwealth,* 123; Eleanore Boswell, *The Restoration Court Stage* (1930; reprint, New York: Benjamin Blom, 1965), 29.

55. Scanlan, "Tennis-Court Theatres," 173, 282, 286.

56. Robert D. Hume's studies lead him to conclude that the best evidence indicates "considerable social, political, and moral diversity" in the audience of the time (*The Rakish Stage: Studies in English Drama 1600–1800* [Carbondale and Edwardsville: Southern Illinois University Press, 1983], 10).

57. Samuel Pepys, 22 July 1663.

58. Montague Summers, ed., *Roscius Anglicanus,* by John Downes (London: Fortune Press, 1929), 165.

59. Antony Aston, *A Brief Supplement to Colley Cibber, Esq; His Lives of the Late Famous Actors and Actresses,* in Robert W. Lowe, ed., *An Apology for the Life of Mr. Colley Cibber,* vol. 2 (London, 1889), 306.

60. Downes, *Roscius Anglicanus,* 1708, 52.

61. Colley Cibber, *Apology,* ed. B. R. S. Fone (Ann Arbor: University of Michigan Press, 1968), 89.

62. Ibid., 83–84.

63. Hugh Hunt considers the entrance of women on the English stage to be the chief ingredient of the new "sensual realism" of Restoration acting ("Restoration Acting," in *Restoration Theatre,* ed. John Russell Brown and Bernard Harris [London, 1965], 182).

64. The year before, moreover, Buckhurst and four others had been charged with killing a man while in pursuit of a band of highwaymen at Stoke Newington.

65. Pepys, *Diary,* 1 July 1663; John Harold Wilson discusses the event at length (*The Court Wits of the Restoration* [Princeton: Princeton University Press, 1948], 40–42).

66. Thorpe, *Poems,* 109–10, assigns the four letters in the group to the 1663–64 period.

67. British Library, Sloane and Add. Mss. 4221; quoted in *Letterbook,* 13.

68. E. Beresford Chancellor, *The Restoration Rakes* (London: Philip Allan & Co., 1924), vol. 2, 131. H. F. Brett-Smith, in *Review of English Studies,* 5 (April 1929):229, points out that MS Birch 4221 (where Chancellor found the account) prints a "______," rather than Chancellor's "kiss." Rosenfeld includes a slightly different version of the story in *Letterbook,* 13–14.

69. "A Session of the Poets," written after *The Man of Mode* was acted in March 1676 (H. F. B. Brett-Smith, *The Dramatic Works of Sir George Etherege* [Oxford, 1927], vol. 1, xxiin), perhaps by Elkanah Settle (see David M. Vieth, *Attribution in Restoration Poetry: A Study of Rochester's "Poems" of 1680* [New Haven and London: Yale University Press, 1963], 30 and *passim*).

70. Joseph Spence, *Observations, Anecdotes, and Characters of Books and Men,* ed. James M. Osborn (Oxford: Clarendon Press, 1966), vol. 2, 281.

71. The authorship of *Poeta de Tristibus* (1682) has been tentatively assigned to Thomas Ward by Harold Love: "The Satirised Characters in *Poeta de Tristibus,*" *Philological Quarterly,* 47 (1968):552. In his edition of *Poeta,* however, Love virtually rejects Ward as author (*Poeta de Tristibus,* Los Angeles: Augustan Reprint Society, Pub. No. 149, 1971, iii–iv).

72. Etherege himself had a similar reputation. In 1680 a satiric poet wrote of him: "Yet there's Sir George, that honest man ne'er fails; / Always of Women Writes and always Rails" (Thorpe, *Poems,* 140).

73. Hume calls such personation "one of the recurrent games played by dramatists in this period" (*The Rakish Stage,* 32).

74. Cited in Brett-Smith, *Dramatic Works,* vol. 1, xx.

75. The date has been found by K. E. Robinson, "A Glance at Rochester in Thomas Durfey's 'Madam Fickle,'" *N & Q,* 22 (June 1975): 364.

76. Foster, *TLS,* 23 February 1922, 124.

77. *Poeta de Tristibus,* ed. Love, 22.

78. Dated by Thorpe between March 1664 and March 1665 (*Poems,* 90).

79. Pepys was surprised to see Buckingham there so soon after his duel with the Earl of Shrewsbury, who would die of his wound the next month: Wilson, *The Court Wits,* 152.

80. Philip H. Highfill et al, *A Biographical Dictionary of Actors, Actresses, Musicians, Dancers . . .* (Carbondale: University of Southern Illinois Press, 1975), vol. 4, 224.

81. Her given name is not known: ibid., vol. 8, 154.

82. Charlene M. Taylor believes that such benefits suggest that actors thought the comedy had excellent drawing power: "Introduction," *She Would If She Could* (Lincoln: University of Nebraska Press, 1971), xiv–xv.

83. Boswell, *RES,* 14.

84. Thomas H. Fujimura, "Etherege at Constantinople," *PMLA,* 72 (June 1956):465–81.

85. A privately owned letter, cited in Brett-Smith, Introduction to *Works,* vol. 1, xx.

86. A "A Prologue Spoken at the Opening of the Duke's New Playhouse," *Poems,* ed. Thorpe, 16–17.

87. Thorpe (*Poems,* 100) found more than twenty appearances of the song in the seventeenth century, and it was set to music by four composers.

88. *The Letters of John Dryden,* ed. Charles E. Ward (1942; reprint, New York: AMS Press, 1965), 10.

89. Rosenfeld, *Letterbook,* 10; see also my article on Etherege's mother in *Notes and Queries,* 263.

90. *The London Stage, Part 1,* 243, suggests this as the date of the premiere on the basis of the licensing date of 3 June 1676.

91. Downes spoke of the play as "being well Cloath'd," (*Roscius Anglicanus,* p. 36).

92. In the introduction to *The Man of Mode* W. B. Carnochan calls attention to the king's attendance at this performance and at another the next month (Lincoln, Neb.: University of Nebraska Press, 1966, x).

93. Downes reports that in *The Conquest of China by the Tartars* he had lain down on his sword in its scabbard rather than falling on the point (p. 35).

94. Leigh created the role of Friar Dominic in the very popular *The Spanish Friar,* first performed in November 1680, and Dryden gave this description of him to the character Gomez (*The Spanish Friar,* 1681 edition, 32). Cibber said that the role of Dominic was "completely written for him" (*Apology,* ed. Fone, 86).

95. Cibber, ed. Fone, 92; the editors of *The London Stage, Part 1,* 243, speculate that Barry did not play Loveit on this occasion, perhaps because she would have been relatively young and inexperienced.

96. Chancellor, *Restoration Rakes,* 127. David M. Vieth calls Dorimant "Rochester's apotheosis" ("Introduction," *The Complete Poems of John Wilmot, Earl of Rochester* [New Haven and London: Yale University Press, 1968], xxvii).

97. Brett-Smith quotes Oldys's MS notes and cites several other attempts at identification ("Introduction," *Dramatic Works,* vol. 1, xxv). Rob-

ert D. Hume refers to a letter by Peter Killigrew, naming Sir Fopling as Villiers and Dorimant as the duke of Monmouth (Spence, *Observations,* vol. 2, 638, Appendix to no. 678, cited in Robert D. Hume, *The Development of English Drama in the Late Seventeenth Century* [Oxford: Clarendon Press, 1976], 91n).

98. Gildon, *The Lives and Characters of the English Dramatick Poets* (London, 1698), 53, quoted in Brett-Smith, *Dramatic Works,* vol. 1, x.

99. Brett-Smith notes that a list of the Duke's pensioners in 1682 includes payment of £100 to Etherege (*Dramatic Works,* vol. 1, xxxii).

100. Ibid., xxviii.

101. Anthony à Wood, *Life and Times,* vol. 2, 477, cited in Rosenfeld, Introduction to *Letterbook,* 15n.

102. John W. Nichol has gathered together most of what is known about Etherege's wife: "Dame Mary Etherege," *Modern Language Notes,* 64 (June 1949):419–22.

103. The fullest source of information about Etherege in Ratisbon is his correspondence, edited by Rosenfeld (*Letterbook*) and by Bracher (*Letters*), and Bracher's three essays in the *Harvard Library Bulletin*: "The Letterbooks of Sir George Etherege," 15 (July 1967):238–45; "Sir George Etherege and His Secretary," 15 (October 1967):331–44; "Etherege as Diplomat," 17 (January 1969):45–60.

104. Letters of 29 December 1687 and 2 September 1688. Etherege had used a similar phrase in *The Comical Revenge,* when Sir Frederick refers to his cast mistress as "household-stuff" (5.5).

105. *Letterbook,* 342.

106. Bracher, "Etherege as Diplomat," 51.

107. A lawsuit filed on 10 May 1687 by Sir George and wife, to recover £300 she had lent before their marriage, indicates that she was then living in the parish of St. Martin's-in-the-Fields: Foster, *N&Q,* 24 December 1927, 456.

108. Letter to the author from Frederick Bracher, 12 September 1973.

109. Rosenfeld (*Letterbook,* 18) points to the Southerne poem, and Gosse (*Seventeenth-Century Studies,* 297) refers to the Dennis pamphlet.

110. Foster, *N&Q,* 31 December 1927, 472.

Chapter Two

1. Prefatory remarks to *The Siege of Rhodes,* cited in Sarup Singh, *The Theory of Drama in the Restoration Period* (Bombay, Calcutta, Madras, New Delhi: Orient Longmans, 1963), 8.

2. Robert D. Hume, Introduction to *The English Mounsieur,* by James Howard, Augustan Reprint Society, nos. 182–83, 1977, i.

3. Louis B. Wright, "The Reading of Plays during the Puritan Revolution," *Huntington Library Bulletin,* no. 6 (1934), 72–108.

4. Gunnar Sorelius, *The Giant Race Before the Flood* (Uppsala: Almqvist & Wiksells, 1966), 172.

5. Robert D. Hume, "Securing a Repertory: Plays on the London Stage 1660–5," in *Poetry and Drama: Essays in Honour of Harold F. Brooks,* ed. Antony Coleman and Antony Hammond, p. 168 (London: Methuen, 1981).

6. John Harrington Smith, *The Gay Couple in Restoration Comedy* (Cambridge: Harvard University Press, 1948), 48.

7. Robert Jordan, "The Extravagant Rake in Restoration Comedy," in *Restoration Literature,* ed. Harold Love, 69–90 (London: Methuen, 1972).

8. Jocelyn Powell, "George Etherege and the Form of a Comedy," in *Restoration Theatre,* ed. Brown and Harris, 45.

9. Ibid.

10. Smith, *The Gay Couple,* 3.

11. David S. Berkeley points out that adoration of woman was a principal theme in Restoration drama ("The Art of 'Whining Love,'" *Studies in Philology* 52 [1955]:478–96).

12. Samuel Johnson, *Johnson on Shakespeare,* ed. Arthur Sherbo, vol. 7 of *The Yale Edition of the Works of Samuel Johnson* (New Haven and London: Yale University Press, 1969), 63.

13. Kathleen Lynch, *The Social Mode of Restoration Comedy* (New York: Macmillan, 1926).

14. Singh, *The Theory of Drama in the Restoration Period,* 2.

Chapter Three

1. Avery and Scouten, "Critical Introduction," *The London Stage, Part 1,* cxxv.

2. Dale Underwood, *Etherege and the Seventeenth-Century Comedy of Manners* (New Haven, Conn.: Yale University Press, 1957), 59.

3. Hume, *The Development of English Drama in the Late Seventeenth Century,* 266.

4. "An Allusion . . . To Horace," *The Complete Poems of John Wilmot, Earl of Rochester,* ed. David M. Vieth (New Haven: Yale University Press, 1968), 122.

5. "A Large Account of the Taste in Poetry, and the Causes of the Degeneracy of It," *Critical Works of John Dennis,* ed. Edward Niles Hooker, 2 vols. (Baltimore: Johns Hopkins Univ. Press, 1939, 1943), vol. 1, 289.

6. Taylor, "Introduction," *She Would If She Could,* xxv.

7. D. R. M. Wilkinson, *The Comedy of Habit: An Essay on the Use of Courtesy Literature in a Study of Restoration Comic Drama* (Leiden: Universitaire Pers, 1964), 92–93.

8. Underwood, *Comedy of Manners,* 59.

9. Powell, "George Etherege and the Form of a Comedy," in *Restoration Theatre,* ed. Brown and Harris, 54.

10. Edmund Gosse, *Seventeenth-Century Studies* (London: Kegan Paul, Trench, 1883), 270–71.

11. William H. Hickerson, "The Significance of James Shirley's Realistic Plays in the History of English Comedy," (Ph.D. diss., University of Michigan, 1932),337, cited in John Wilcox, *The Relation of Molière to Restoration Comedy,* 79 (New York: Columbia University Press, 1938).

12. Wilcox, *The Relation of Molière to Resolution Comedy,* 78–79; Underwood, *Comedy of Manners,* 64. Courtall calls her a "haggard" (3.1), meaning a wild female hawk rather than an ugly woman.

13. Reba Wilkinson, "Mirrors of Men's Fears: The Court Satires on Women," *Restoration* 3 (Fall 1979):47.

14. William Congreve, "Concerning Humour in Comedy (1695)," in *Critical Essays of the Seventeenth Century,* ed. J. E. Spingarn, vol. 3, 246 (Oxford, 1909; reprint, Bloomington, Ind.: Indiana University Press, 1957).

15. David Berkeley, "*Préciosité* and the Restoration Comedy of Manners," *Huntington Library Quarterly* 18 (February 1955):112.

Chapter Four

1. John Barnard, "Point of View in *The Man of Mode,*" *Essays in Criticism* 24 (October 1984):285.

2. Ibid.

3. Ibid., 290.

4. David Mann, *Sir George Etherege: A Reference Guide* (Boston: G. K. Hall, 1981).

5. Wilkinson, *The Comedy of Habit,* 122

6. Underwood, *Comedy of Manners,* 73.

7. Ibid., 92. Cf. also Allan Rodway, who argues that the play offers no standard of values: "Etherege, Wycherley, Congreve, Farquhar," *English Comedy* (London: Chatto & Windus, 1975), 124–43.

8. William Hazlitt, "On Cowley, Butler, Suckling, Etherege, etc.," Lecture 3 in *Lectures on the English Comic Writers* (London, 1819), 130.

9. Kenneth Muir, *The Comedy of Manners* (London: Hutchinson, 1970), 34.

10. John Barnard, introduction to his edition of *The Man of Mode* (London: Ernest Behn, 1979), xxx–xxxi.

11. Vivian de Sola Pinto's review of *The Works of Sir George Etherege,* ed. H. F. B. Brett-Smith, 2 vols. (Oxford, 1927), in *Review of English Studies* 4 (1928):347.

12. Wandalie Henshaw, "Sir Fopling Flutter or the Key to *The Man of Mode,*" *Essays in Theatre* 3 (1985):105.

13. "A Case of Restoration: Terry Hands and Timothy O'Brien Talk to Robert Waterhouse," *Plays and Players* 19 (November 1971):14–15. Harry William Pedicord has recently reported on a 1984 English production of *The*

Man of Mode at which the audience accorded Sir Fopling his greatest laugh during the looking-glass episode in Dorimant's lodging, a scene with decided possibilities for farcical treatment: "An Etherege in an Orange Tree," *Restoration* 8 (Fall 1984):59–60.

14. C. D. Cecil, "'Une espèce d'eloquence abrégée': The Idealized Speech of Restoration Comedy," *Etudes Anglaises* 19 (1966):15–25.

15. Barnard, "Point of View in *The Man of Mode*," 302.

16. Thomas Hobbes, *Leviathan* (Oxford: Clarendon Press, 1909), 123.

17. Susan Staves, *Studies in English Literature* 22 (Summer 1982): 413–28.

18. Derek Hughes, "Play and Passion in *The Man of Mode*," *Comparative Drama* 15 (1981):236.

19. Barnard, "Point of View in *The Man of Mode*, 303–5.

Chapter Five

1. Wilson, *The Court Wits*, 111.

2. Reported by Edmund Gosse, *Seventeenth-Century Studies* 1883, 276.

3. Preface to *Examen Poeticum* (London, 1693), as quoted in Thorpe, "Preface," *Poems*, vi.

4. Ibid., vi–vii.

5. Purvis E. Boyette, "The Songs of George Etherege," *Studies in English Literature, 1500–1900* 6 (1966):419.

6. Thorpe, *Poems*, 90–91.

7. The phrase, coined by the earl of Rochester, appears in his satire "Timon" (1674). Cf. Vieth, ed., *Complete Poems of Rochester*, 70.

8. Earl Miner, *The Restoration Mode from Milton to Dryden* (Princeton, N.J.: Princeton University Press, 1974), 377.

9. The bulk of Etherege's correspondence exists in three manuscript collections: The Middleton Papers in the British Museum, the unofficial Letterbook in the British Museum, and the official letterbooks at the Houghton Library, Harvard. Published editions include *The Letterbook of Sir George Etherege*, ed. Sybil Rosenfeld (London, 1927), and *Letters of Sir George Etherege*, ed. Frederick Bracher (Berkeley and Los Angeles, 1974). Three articles by Bracher explore the Ratisbon period, all printed in the *Harvard Library Bulletin:* "The Letterbooks of Sir George Etherege," 15 (July 1967), 238–45; "Sir George Etherege and His Secretary," 15 (October 1967), 331–44; "Etherege as Diplomat," 17 (January, 1969),45–60. See also my lengthy review of *Letters* in *Modern Philology* 73 (November 1975), 194–200.

10. BM ADD MS 41836, the Middleton Papers, vol. 1.

11. Ibid.

12. Bracher, "Sir George Etherege and His Secretary," 341.

13. Etherege wrote Dryden on 26 September 1686, 30 January 1687, and perhaps again in early January 1687 (Dryden wrote that he had received

a letter about 24 January; if we allow two weeks for that letter to reach London, it must have been sent by Etherege about 10 January 1687). Cf. *Letters, passim.*

14. Letter of 16 February 1687, *Letters,* 276–77.

Chapter Six

1. *The Complete Poems of John Wilmot, Earl of Rochester,* ed. Vieth, 70. Except as indicated in the notes to follow, I have relied for citations on David D. Mann's *Sir George Etherege: A Reference Guide.*

2. [Gerard] Langbaine, *An Account of the English Dramatick Poets* (Oxford: printed by L. L. for George West and Henry Clements, 1691), 187; Gildon, *The Lives and Characters of the English Dramatick Poets,* 53–54.

3. Edmund Gosse, "Sir George Etherege: A Neglected Chapter of English Literature," *Cornhill Magazine* 43 (1881):284–304.

4. John Palmer, *The Comedy of Manners* (London: G. Bell, 1913), 21.

5. Underwood, *Comedy of Manners,* 73.

6. N. J. Rigaud, *George Etherege, Dramaturge de la Restauration Anglaise* (Lille and Paris, 1980), 2:639–42.

7. Hume, *The Development of English Drama,* 89, 91, 95.

8. Robert D. Hume, *The Rakish Stage* (Carbondale and Edwardsville: Southern Illinois University Press, 1983), 143, 166.

Selected Bibliography

PRIMARY SOURCES

1. First and Modern Editions of Individual Plays

The Comical Revenge; or, Love in a Tub. London: Printed for Henry Herringman, 1664.

She wou'd if she cou'd, A Comedy. London: Printed for H. Herringman, 1668.

She Would If She Could. Edited by Charlene M. Taylor. Lincoln: University of Nebraska Press, 1971.

The Man of Mode, or, Sir Fopling Flutter. London: Printed by J. Macock for Henry Herringman, 1676.

The Man of Mode. Edited by W. B. Carnochan. Lincoln: University of Nebraska Press, 1966.

The Man of Mode; or, Sir Fopling Flutter. Edited by John Barnard. London: Ernest Behn, 1979; New York: W. W. Norton, 1979.

2. Collected Editions of Plays

The Works of Sir George Etherege: Containing His Plays and Poems. London: Printed for H. H. and sold by J. Tonson, 1704. The title pages of *She Would If She Could* and *The Man of Mode* are dated 1703.

The Works of Sir George Etherege: Containing His Plays and Poems. London: Printed for Jacob Tonson, 1715. Reprints in 1723 and 1735.

The Works of Sir George Etheredge, Plays and Poems. Edited by A. Wilson Verity. London: John C. Nimmo, 1888.

The Dramatic Works of Sir George Etherege. Edited by H. F. B. Brett-Smith. 2 vols. 1927. Reprint. St.Clair Shores, Mich.: Scholarly Press, 1971.

The Plays of Sir George Etherege. Edited by Michael Cordner. Cambridge, England, and New York: Cambridge University Press, 1982. The first collected edition since Brett-Smith. Modernized, with an excellent introduction.

3. Poems

The Poems of Sir George Etherege. Edited by James Thorpe. Princeton: Princeton University Press, 1963. Prints 31 authentic poems.

4. Letters

The Letterbook of Sir George Etherege. Edited by Sybil Rosenfeld. 1928. Reprint. New York: Benjamin Blom, 1971. Edition of the secret letterbook kept in Ratisbon by secretary Hugo Hughes.

Letters of Sir George Etherege. Edited by Frederick Bracher. Berkeley: University of California Press, 1974. Prints the most important letters from the Middleton Papers, the official letterbook, and the secret letterbook kept by secretary Hughes.

SECONDARY SOURCES

1. Bibliography

Mann, David D. *Sir George Etherege: A Reference Guide.* Boston: G. K. Hall, 1981.

2. Books

Birdsall, Virginia Ogden. *Wild Civility: The English Comic Spirit on the Restoration Stage.* Bloomington, Ind.: Indiana University Press, 1970. The comedies of Etherege, Wycherley, and Congreve celebrate the libertinism of a rake-hero of intellect and spirit.

Bruce, Donald. *Topics of Restoration Comedy.* New York: St. Martins Press, 1974. Etherege's plays are in the tradition of Middleton's comedies; Dorimant is a "Petronian Epicure."

Downes, John. *Roscius Anglicanus.* London: H. Playford, 1708. History of the Restoration theaters by a firsthand observer.

Fujimura, Thomas H. *The Restoration Comedy of Wit.* Princeton: Princeton University Press, 1952. Argues that the comedy of wit gives "freedom and pleasure."

Gosse, Edmund. *Seventeenth-Century Studies.* London: Kegan Paul, Trench, 1883. Gosse participated in the discovery of Hughes's secret letterbook; his influential study added Etherege to the canon of great Restoration comedy.

Harbage, Alfred. *Cavalier Drama.* New York: Modern Language Association, 1936. Argues that the heroic plays of the Restoration continue the Cavalier mode and are thus of English origin.

Harris, Brice. *Charles Sackville, Sixth Earl of Dorset: Patron and Poet of the Restoration.* Urbana: University of Illinois Press, 1940. Life and career of Etherege's good friend.

Highfill, Philip H. et al. *Biographical Dictionary of Actors, Actresses, Musicians, Dancers, Managers, and Other Stage Personnel in London, 1660–1800.* Carbondale and Edwardsville: Southern Illinois University Press, 1973–. Volumes 1–10 (M'Intosh to Nash) have been published.

Holland, Norman N. *The First Modern Comedies: The Significance of Etherege, Wycherley, and Congreve.* Cambridge: Harvard University Press, 1959. Explores the discrepancy between appearance and nature in eleven plays; notes that discrepancy is at the heart of every phase of Restoration life.

The action of *The Man of Mode* is "a great and meaningless social game."

Holland, Peter. *The Ornament of Action: Text and Performance in Restoration Comedy.* Cambridge, England: Cambridge University Press, 1979. Plays are discussed in relation to performance and scenic conventions.

Hotson, Leslie. *The Commonwealth and Restoration Stage.* Cambridge: Harvard University Press, 1928. The background of Restoration comedy, based on over 120 lawsuits relating to stage history.

Hume, Robert D. *The Development of English Drama in the Late Seventeenth Century.* Oxford: Clarendon Press, 1976. Basing his judgments on the reading of five hundred Restoration plays, Hume concludes that Etherege was not the norm of the time and that later comedy does not follow his lead.

———. *The Rakish Stage: Studies in English Drama, 1600–1800.* Carbondale and Edwardsville: Southern Illinois University Press, 1983. "There is no instance in late seventeenth-century comedy in which 'libertinism' is presented both seriously and favorably," and "I have never found a play which seemed to me genuinely to attack marriage as an institution or to envisage any serious alternative."

The London Stage, 1660–1800. Five parts in 11 vols. Carbondale: Southern Illinois University Press, 1960–1968. Edited by various hands. Part 1, 1660–1700, is useful as a record of performances during Etherege's lifetime.

Lynch, Kathleen. *The Social Mode of Restoration Comedy.* New York: Macmillan Co., 1926. An important early study of the milieu of Restoration comedy, especially the chapter about the précieuse tradition 1642–1664.

Mann, David D., ed. *A Concordance to the Plays and Poems of Sir George Etherege.* Westport, Conn.: Greenwood Press, 1985.

Nicoll, Allardyce. *A History of Restoration Drama.* Cambridge: Cambridge University Press, 1923. Definitive and frequently reprinted study of later seventeenth-century drama.

Palmer, John. *The Comedy of Manners.* London: G. Bell, 1913. Pioneer study of Restoration comedy; argues that manners comedy began with Etherege.

Perry, Henry Ten Eyck. *The Comic Spirit in Restoration Drama: Studies in the Comedy of Etherege, Wycherley, Congreve, Vanbrugh, and Farquhar.* New Haven: Yale University Press, 1925. The love chase is central to Etherege's three plays; their male protagonists are very similar.

Singh, Sarup. *The Theory of Drama in the Restoration Period.* Bombay, Calcutta, Madras, New Delhi: Orient Longmans, 1963. Critical theory of the Restoration drama as expressed in dedications, prologues, etc. Chapters on the heroic play, rhyme, tragicomedy, comedy of manners, and others.

Smith, John Harrington. *The Gay Couple in Restoration Comedy*. Cambridge: Harvard University Press, 1948. Places Etherege's first two plays with the gay-couple comedy; *The Man of Mode* belongs with cynical comedy.

Sorelius, Gunnar. *"The Giant Race Before the Flood": Pre-Restoration Drama on the Stage and in the Criticism of the Restoration*. Uppsala: Almqvist & Wiksells, 1966. Studies the drama of the pre-Restoration period and the relationships between the old drama and the new. Discusses changing conditions of the theater 1660–1700.

Underwood, Dale. *Etherege and the Seventeenth Century Comedy of Manners*. New Haven: Yale University Press, 1957. Argues that the form and meaning of the comedies reflect the juxtaposing of two opposing sets of traditions: Christian humanism and libertinism.

Wilcox, John. *The Relation of Molière to Restoration Comedy*. New York: Columbia University Press, 1938. Etherege is found to have been quite free from the influence of Molière.

Wilkinson, D. R. M. *The Comedy of Habit: An Essay on the Use of Courtesy Literature in a Study of Restoration Comic Drama*. Leiden: Universitaire Pers, 1964. Uses the literature to examine the wit and characterization of the gallant, especially in the plays of Etherege and Wycherley.

Wilson, John Harold. *The Court Wits of the Restoration*. Princeton: Princeton University Press, 1948. About the lives of the courtiers, with readings of Etherege's three plays.

3. Articles

Barnard, John. "Point of View in *The Man of Mode*." *Essays in Criticism*, 34 (1984):285–308. Emphasizes the aristocratic and modish nature of the audience in interpreting the meaning of the comedy. The ending shifts attention from Dorimant to Fopling, thus allowing the play to end as entertainment.

Bell, Robert. "The Comedies of Etherege." *Fortnightly Review* 3 (1866): 298–316. Enthusiastic review of all three plays; does not manage to rescue Etherege's reputation.

Berkeley, David S. "The Art of 'Whining' Love." *Studies in Philology* 52 (1955):478–96. A conventional and formal method of lovemaking in the "romantick stile," codified from the romances.

———. "The Penitent Rake in Restoration Comedy." *Modern Philology* 49 (May 1952):223–33. On the reformation of rakes, usually by semidivine ladies.

———. "*Préciosité* and the Restoration Comedy of Manners. *Huntington Library Quarterly* 18 (February 1955):109–28. Reviews the historical background of this form of ceremonious social intercourse, against which patterns of courtship in manners comedy had meaning.

Berman, Ronald. "The Comic Passions of *The Man of Mode*." *Studies in En-*

glish Literature, 1500–1900 10 (1970):459–68. The attitudes in the play depend on the values found in Waller's poetry.

Boswell, Eleanore. "Sir George Etherege." *Review of English Studies* 7 (1931):207–9. Adds new information about Etherege's life, especially in 1668 and while in Ratisbon.

Boyette, Purvis E. "The Songs of George Etherege." *Studies in English Literature, 1500–1900* 6 (1966):409–19. Examines the use of songs in the three comedies; calls him the best songwriter of the playwrights of the time.

Bracher, Frederick. "Etherege as Diplomat." *Harvard Library Bulletin* 17 (January 1969):45–60. Essential study of Etherege at Ratisbon, based on the letterbooks.

———. "Etherege at Clement's Inn." *Huntington Library Quarterly* 43 (Spring 1980):127–34. Examines Etherege's probable life as a law student based on his name in the Clement's Inn Admissions Book.

———. "The Letterbooks of Sir George Etherege." *Harvard Library Bulletin* 15 (July 1967):238–45. Clarifies the record of Etherege's correspondence.

———. "Sir George Etherege and His Secretary." *Harvard Library Bulletin* 15 (October 1967):331–44. Studies the career of Hugo Hughes, Etherege's secretary at Ratisbon.

Brown, Laura S. "The Divided Plot: Tragicomic Form in the Restoration." *ELH* 57 (1980):67–79. *The Comical Revenge* exemplifies the typical tragicomic division into serious and comic actions.

Bruder, C. Harry. "Women in the Comedies of Sir George Etherege." *Papers of the Arkansas Philological Association* 10, no. 2 (1984):1–11. Harriet is the culmination of an increasingly mature treatment of women in the comedies.

Cecil, C. D. "Libertine and Précieux Elements in Restoration Comedy." *Essays in Criticism* 9 (1959):239–53. Comedy attempts to realize an ideal personality by ridiculing extremes of refined conduct.

———. "'Une espèce d'éloquence abrégée': The Idealized Speech of Restoration Comedy." *Études Anglaises* 19 (1966):15–25. Restoration comedy reflects a high interest in the refinement of conversational expression.

Corman, Brian. "Interpreting and Misinterpreting *The Man of Mode*." *Papers on Language and Literature* 13 (1977):35–53. "The relationship between Dorimant and Harriet" propels them "almost irreversibly toward the marriage one expects at the end of the comedy."

———. "What Is Restoration Drama?" *University of Toronto Quarterly* 48 (Fall 1978):53–66. Review of Hume's "essential study" *The Development of the English Drama in the Late Seventeenth Century*. Considers it the most trustworthy account of what happened on the English stage during the period but argues that what is meant by development remains unclear.

Davies, Paul C. "The State of Nature and the State of War: A Reconsideration of *The Man of Mode.*" *University of Toronto Quarterly* 39 (1969):53–62. Concludes that it is "an uncompromisingly tough and realistic play, at the conclusion of which no one's character has changed. . . ."

Foster, Dorothy. Articles under various titles: *Times* (London) *Literary Supplement* (16 February 1922), 108; *TLS* (23 February 1922), 124; *Notes and Queries* (6 May 1922), 341–44; *N & Q* (13 May 1922), 362–65; *N & Q* (27 May 1922), 414; *N & Q* (10 December 1927), 417–19; *N & Q* (17 December 1927), 435–40); *N & Q* (24 December 1927), 454–59; *N & Q* (31 December 1927), 472–78; *N & Q* (14 January 1928), 28; *TLS* (31 May 1928), 412; *Review of English Studies* 8 (October 1932), 458–59. Foster's extensive contributions to the study of Etherege's life and career are based essentially on the lawsuit material of 1656–57.

Fujimura, Thomas. "Etherege at Constantinople." *PMLA* 72 (June 1956):465–81. Examines Etherege's three years abroad as secretary to Sir Daniel Harvey, ambassador to Turkey.

Hayman, John G. "Dorimant and the Comedy of a Man of Mode." *Modern Language Quarterly* 30 (June 1969):183–97. Dorimant fails to fulfill the requirements of polite society by turning all to selfish ends.

Heilman, Robert B. "Some Fops and Some Versions of Foppery." *ELH* 49 (1982):363–95. Wycherley's Dapperwit is the first fop of character; Sir Fopling "presents the new fop in his first full development."

Hughes, Derek. "Play and Passion in *The Man of Mode.*" *Comparative Drama* 15 (Fall 1981):231–57. The comedy juxtaposes "serious and comic responses to the same experiences."

Hume, Robert D. "Elizabeth Barry's First Roles and the Cast of *The Man of Mode. Theatre History Studies* 5 (1985): 16–19. There is no reason to doubt that Barry played Loveit in March 1676.

———. "Securing a Repertory, Plays on the London Stage 1660–5." In *Poetry and Drama: Essays in Honour of Harold F. Brooks,* edited by Antony Coleman and Antony Hammond, 156–72. London: Methuen, 1981. Examines the competition between Davenant and Killigrew for plays. "With *The Indian Queen, The English Mounsieur,* and *The Comical Revenge* in 1663 and early 1664 we find a new tone and attitude."

Huseboe, Arthur R. "The Mother of Sir George Etherege." *Notes and Queries* 20 (June 1975):262–64. The parish registers of Old Windsor provide information about the dates of birth of Mary Powney Etherege and her brothers and sister.

Isaacs, J. "Sir George Etherege at Constantinople." *Times* (London) *Literary Supplement.* 10 November 1921, p. 734. Prints Etherege's Constantinople letter for the first time.

Jordan, Robert. "The Extravagant Rake in Restoration Comedy." In *Resto-*

ration Literature, edited by Harold Love, 69–90. London: Methuen, 1972. Contrasts the extravagant and the gentleman rake; Dorimant is one of the latter, noted for control and smooth social manner.

Kaul, A. N. "The Inverted Abstractions of Restoration Comedy." In *The Action of English Comedy,* 90–130. New Haven: Yale University Press, 1971. Calls *The Man of Mode* "perhaps the most brilliant and ruthless of Restoration comedies."

Kishi, Tetsuo. "George Etherege and the Destiny of Restoration Comedy." In *English Criticism in Japan,* edited by Earl Miner, 156–69. Tokyo: University of Tokyo Press, 1972. What looks like disunity in *Love in a Tub* is really the result of an ambivalent attitude on the part of the author toward heroic virtue.

Krause, David. "The Defaced Angel: A Concept of Satanic Grace in Etherege's *The Man of Mode.*" *Drama Survey* 7 (Winter 1968–69):87–103. Dorimant is comically tamed by a woman even tougher and more self-controlled than he.

Nichol, John W. "Dame Mary Etherege." *Modern Language Notes* 64 (June 1949):419–22. Gathers together most of what is known about Etherege's wife.

Oldys, William. "Sir George Etherege." *Biographia Britannica* (London, 1750), 3:1841. First biographical account based on interviews with acquaintances of Etherege.

Pedicord, Harry William. "An Etherege in an Orange Tree." *Restoration* 8 (Fall 1984):58–61. *The Man of Mode* at the Orange Tree Theatre, Richmond, Surrey.

———. "Revivals of Restoration Comedies in London." *Restoration* 3 (Fall 1979):66–68. About a revival of *She Would If She Could.*

Pinto, Vivian de Sola. Review of *The Works of Sir George Etherege,* edited by H. F. B. Brett-Smith. *Review of English Studies* 4 (1928):341–49. Authoritative review of the *Works,* with a sketch of Etherege's career and importance.

Powell, Jocelyn. "George Etherege and the Form of a Comedy." In *Restoration Theatre,* edited by John Russell Brown and Bernard Harris, 43–69. London: Edward Arnold; New York: St. Martin's Press, 1965. Etherege's plays show increasing economy of dramatic means; he moves from the comedy of judgment to the comedy of experience.

Rodway, Allan. "Etherege, Wycherley, Congreve, Farquhar." *English Comedy: Its Role and Nature from Chaucer to the Present Day,* 124–43. London: Chatto & Windus, 1975. Etherege's characters take nothing seriously; the comedy encourages laughter "neither with, nor at, but *about.*"

Rosenfeld, Sybil. "Sir George Etherege in Ratisbon." *Review of English Studies* 10 (1934):177–89. Examines Etherege's letters among the Middleton Papers at the British Museum.

Sherbo, Arthur. "A Note on *The Man of Mode.*" *Modern Language Notes* 64 (May 1949):343–44. Sir Fopling's calling his equipage is echoed from Molière's *Les Précieuses Ridicules.*

Staves, Susan. "A Few Kind Words for the Fop." *Studies in English Literature, 1500–1900* 22 (1982):413–28. Sir Fopling and his descendants possess what many people today would call desirable masculine virtues.

Thompson, James. "Lying and Dissembling in the Restoration." *Restoration* 6 (Spring 1982):11–19. Dorimant is a dissembler but not a dishonorable deceiver.

Traugott, John. "The Rake's Progress from Court to Comedy: A Study in Comic Form." *Studies in English Literature, 1500–1900* 6 (Summer 1966):381–407. "The rake is a creature of the Restoration's powerful nostalgia for the pompous virtues of the heroic play." "Dorimant" means golden lover.

Waterhouse, Robert. "A Case of Restoration: Terry Hands and Timothy O'Brien Talk to Robert Waterhouse." *Plays and Players* 19 (November 1971):14–16, 84. Discussion of the Royal Shakespeare Company's attempt to put *The Man of Mode* into a contemporary setting.

Zimbardo, Rose A. "Of Women, Comic Imitation of Nature, and Etherege's *The Man of Mode.*" *Studies in English Literature, 1500–1900* 21 (Summer 1981):373–87. Harriet serves as "an instrument of nature" to undermine the heroic pretensions of the protagonist Dorimant.

4. Unpublished Dissertations

Beless, Rosemary June. "Reflections of the Law in the Comedies of Etherege, Wycherley, and Congreve." Ph.D. diss., University of Utah, 1977. Useful study of legal terminology and concepts in the comedies.

Meindl, Vincenz. *Sir George Etheredge.* 1901. Reprint. London: Johnson Reprint Company Limited, 1964. Austrian thesis (in German); includes a brief biography, a sketch of the times, chapters on Restoration Theater and on the three plays.

Rigaud, N. J. *George Etherege, Dramaturge de la Restauration Anglaise.* Lille: Atelier Reproduction des Theses Université de Lille III; Paris: Diffusion Librairie Honore Champion, 1980. 2 vols. Lengthy study (947 pp.) in French of Etherege's milieu and his plays. Rigaud finds numerous echoes and analogues in Jacobean and contemporary Restoration drama. Chapters on the milieu, intellectual life, theater, E's career, and on each of the plays. No new information from French sources about his years in Paris 1689–1692.

Scanlan, Elizabeth. "Tennis-Court Theatres and the Duke's Playhouse, 1661–1671." Ph.D. diss., Columbia University, 1952. Details about the theater in which Etherege's first two comedies were performed.

Index

DATE DUE
